Teacher's Handbook

SRA

Reading LABORATORY®

1b

McGraw Hill

SRA

mheducation.com/prek-12

Send all inquiries to:
McGraw-Hill Education
8787 Orion Place
Columbus, OH 43240

ISBN: 978-0-07-702357-7
MHID: 0-07-702357-9

Printed in the United States of America.

5 6 7 8 9 LHN 24 23

Table of Contents

5 Preface to the 2020 Edition

7 Overview: Getting to Know the Program

10 Materials

12 Recommended Schedule and Teaching Plans

13 Session 1
Student Placement Starter Stories

18 Session 2
Reading Laboratory Introduction

20 Session 3
Power Builder Procedures

22 Session 4
Power Builders: Independent Use

25 Session 5
Power Builders: Comprehension and SQR Formula

27 Session 6
Power Builders: More Comprehension Strategies

29 Session 7
Power Builders: Individual Conferences

33 Session 8
Final Evaluation

34 Appendix A
Answers to Frequently Asked Questions

37 Appendix B
Power Builder Titles

43 Appendix C
Comprehension and Word-Study Skills Charts

Table of Contents

55 Appendix D Student Resources

56 Home Connection Letter

57 Starter Story 1

61 Starter Story 2

65 Starter Story 3

69 Starter Story 4

73 Starter Story 5

77 Starter Story 6

81 Record Page

82 Progress Charts

94 Answer Key

Preface to the 2020 Edition

A Wealth of Good Reading

For more than sixty years, teachers have been aware of the strengths of *SRA Reading Laboratory*—how it provides individualized skills instruction, permits independent work, promotes students' sense of responsibility, and lets each student move at his or her own rate, according to individual ability. However, there is another aspect of *SRA Reading Laboratory* that deserves to be stressed: the great quantity of good reading passages to be found.

The reading selections in *SRA Reading Laboratory* are by no means just sterile skills exercises. They are a balanced collection of fiction and nonfiction short stories and articles that students actually enjoy reading. In addition, they are sources of a great deal of incidental learning as well—about plants, animals, history, science, technology, discovery, fine arts, social institutions, sports, and different cultures.

Students don't just learn to read better by using *SRA Reading Laboratory*; they discover what it means to become readers. They gain pleasure, information, and—if the ultimate goal succeeds—a lifelong love of reading in all kinds of subject areas. They learn to read for a variety of purposes, and they discover what it is to read in a wide range of content areas. Good reading is not just an incidental aspect of *SRA Reading Laboratory* but one of its principal elements and strengths.

Every new edition of *SRA Reading Laboratory* is updated and improved over previous editions. In this 2020 edition, many of the *Power Builder* selections have been replaced with brand-new selections, while other selections have been edited to bring them up to date. The nonfiction reading selections are enhanced by colorful photographs, and the fictional stories incorporate engaging illustrations to promote comprehension and reading enjoyment.

Equitable Educational Resources

The collection of readings exposes students to a balance of fiction and nonfiction genres, such as classic literature, folktales, fantasy, and informational text. In addition, the readings focus on a variety of topics, including science, technology, history, and cultures. The emphasis on student choice and engagement in ***SRA Reading Laboratory*** provides students with essential knowledge and academic vocabulary which is just as important for a literate reader as are developing the skills of decoding, vocabulary, and structural analysis.

Virtually any interesting reading materials can be used to build skills, but materials relating to our tremendous diversity among cultures will help to build a more equitable education for all students. The ***Power Builder*** selections enable students to gain an understanding and appreciation of worldwide settings, lifestyles, problems, and perspectives.

Social and Emotional Learning

In reading the ***Power Builder*** selections, not only will students find plentiful entertainment, but they also will learn about the consequences of greed and the rewards of kindness, generosity, and honesty. They will read true stories about the accomplishments and struggles of all kinds of people throughout history.

As you use ***SRA Reading Laboratory***, incorporate the following suggestions in your classroom to instill core social and emotional competencies in students.

- Create a continuously nurturing environment for learning but encourage individual student goal setting and progress. Reward positive behavior and help students feel ownership over their own progress.
- Integrate social and emotional skill building by giving students the opportunity for self-reflection on their own reading process.
- Communicate early and often with students and their families. Have students present their progress at parent-teacher conferences. Encourage students to track their progress and to discuss their difficulties and their successes.
- Empower students to become self-directed learners. Talk about growth mindset and make sure students understand how they can work to improve their skills. Encourage students to persist when faced with difficult tasks.

Overview: Getting to Know the Program

Methods and Goals

As a teacher, you know that students differ in how fast they learn as well as in how much they learn. A typical classroom has many levels of learning. Therefore, there is a great need for a systematic way of accommodating all those levels at the same time. *SRA Reading Laboratory* does precisely that.

The program meets the differing needs of students by providing multilevel learning materials in one classroom package. It is a complete system offering individualized reading opportunities to all your students. You need no additional materials or teaching assistance to operate it. In fact, it basically operates itself. After some initial training, students manage their own learning. They work independently, score their own work, and keep accurate accounts of their own progress.

The reading materials and associated skills exercises in any one *Reading Laboratory* are organized into a series of color-designated difficulty levels that range above and below the average for that grade or age group. The student who reads below grade level finds material that he or she can read right away. This removes the frustration of trying to read and understand material that is too difficult. At the same time, the more advanced student finds materials suited to his or her abilities. This removes the potential boredom that comes with reading materials that are too easy. Students progress according to their own abilities and at whatever pace is appropriate to each one.

You begin using the program in your classroom by working through a series of six Starter Sessions to determine the color level and corresponding Lexile® range in which each student should start. Even if your students have used the program before, it is important to begin each school year with the Starter Sessions and other introductory procedures in order to ensure accurate placement after periods of break time.

Students work individually and chart their progress. Once a week, you may want to have a brief individual conference with each student. By studying the progress charts with the student, you can help the student evaluate his or her work. Then you and the student can decide together whether he or she is ready to move to the next color level.

Goals of SRA Reading Laboratory

1 To develop comprehension, vocabulary, word analysis, and study skills

2 To reinforce specific skills to help students become proficient readers

3 To interest students in reading and to enlarge their specific knowledge, using a wide array of quality fiction and nonfiction selections

4 To develop independent readers with strong comprehension skills, endurance, and confidence

5 To develop the sense of personal responsibility as students take charge of their own learning

Teachers are often surprised to see how much responsibility students can take for their own learning. The more you work with multilevel teaching and learning, the more opportunities you will find for building one-to-one relationships with your students. You will also see how students' self-esteem grows with learning.

The goals of *SRA Reading Laboratory* go well beyond mere skills learning, although skills learning is certainly an important part of the whole. Five main goals are served by the various learning materials in *SRA Reading Laboratory* and by the educational method and philosophy of the multilevel system.

See Appendix D for a listing of specific comprehension and word-study skills.

If you wish to review in detail the reading skills on which the program is focused, turn to the Comprehension and Word-Study Skills Charts in Appendix D of this handbook. There you can see at a glance the specific skills presented in each reading level and in each *Power Builder* within each level.

Getting the Most Out of the Program

A clear understanding of the program will help ensure that you and your students derive maximum benefit from *SRA Reading Laboratory's* pedagogical design. Special emphasis is given to these points at the outset so that they will not be overlooked.

1 *SRA Reading Laboratory* is a system that has been carefully structured for teaching and developing essential skills and beneficial attitudes in an orderly and purposeful method. When treated as a regularly scheduled part of the classroom routine, the laboratory offers you an organized, systematic program that can significantly improve reading skills, study habits, and feelings of personal responsibility.

When practice periods are kept close together, there is carryover learning from day to day.

2 *SRA Reading Laboratory* is a flexible program that can be easily implemented to fit into a variety of school calendars and schedules. One suggestion that has been proven effective is to use the program over a fairly concentrated period of time instead of being widely spaced across the entire school year. The recommended schedule on page 12 calls for eight sessions (twenty to forty minutes long) spaced closely together during the training phase and then followed by a phase in which students use the program materials independently. When practice periods are kept close together, there is carryover learning from one day to the next. When practice periods are spaced too far apart, carryover is lessened, and students tend to forget not only the information learned but even the procedures to follow.

3 It is not intended that every student work his or her way through *all* the ***Power Builders*** in a level or that a student work the ***Power Builders*** in strict sequence. Instead, a student selects (or is given)* ***Power Builders*** in *random* sequence from his or her assigned level; as soon as the student's scores show adequate progress (as discussed on pages 29–32), the student advances to the next color level. Thus, the number of ***Power Builders*** that any student will work in a particular level will vary according to his or her abilities and learning rate. A typical student should probably complete at least four ***Power Builders*** in a level; others may do eight or ten. Some students may require practice with all ***Power Builders*** in a level before moving on.

Students will complete different numbers of ***Power Builders*** depending on their own progress.

4 After the training phase, it is a good idea to begin holding weekly conferences with each student to review his or her progress. You are strongly encouraged to make these conferences mutual consultations in which you and the student decide together whether it is time to move to a new level. Getting students accustomed to taking responsibility for their own learning progress is important if you are to realize the full potential of ***SRA Reading Laboratory*** as not just a builder of skills but of self-image and self-confidence as well.

Encourage students to take responsibility for their own learning.

Although free choice of* ***Power Builders* *by individuals is consistent with the laboratory's purpose and design, the procedure described later in this handbook eliminates individual choice to reduce the confusion resulting from traffic to and from the laboratory box. Student helpers or group leaders can hand out the Progress Charts, Record Pages, and the* ***Power Builders,*** *giving each student any* ***Power Builder*** *that he or she has not yet read in the assigned color level. In this system, the group leaders also collect the materials at the end of the period and refile the* ***Power Builders*** *in the laboratory box. Whether to use this group-leader system or to let each student select his or her materials from the box is up to you.*

Materials

SRA Reading Laboratory contains the following materials:

Teacher's Handbook

The *Teacher's Handbook* contains an overview of ***SRA Reading Laboratory*** and provides teaching plans for using the program to its maximum advantage. The separate appendixes of the References and Resources section provide detailed information about program selections, skills, and procedures.

The Student Resources section includes a Home Connection letter that should be copied and given to students to take home to provide information to parents and guardians about the program. In addition, the Student Resources section includes the Starter Stories, Record Pages, and Progress Charts. You will copy and distribute these materials as needed.

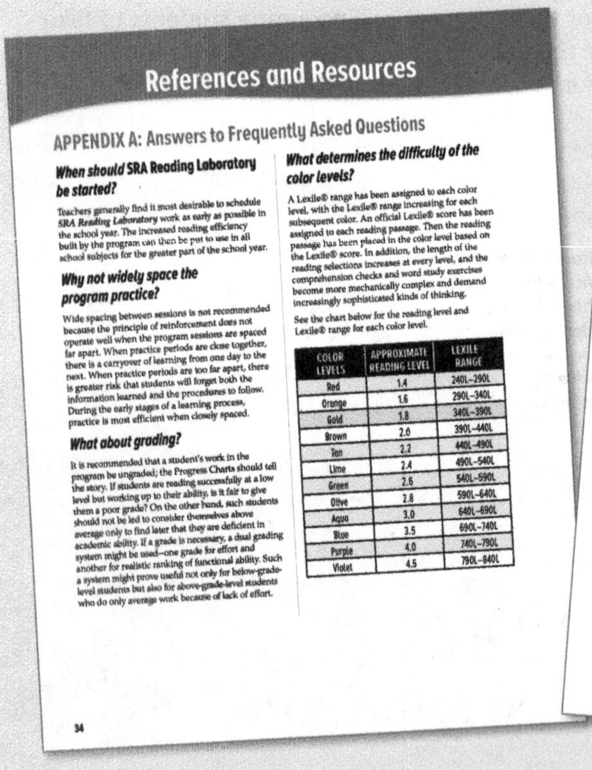

References and Resources

APPENDIX A: Answers to Frequently Asked Questions

When should SRA Reading Laboratory be started?

Teachers generally find it most desirable to schedule *SRA Reading Laboratory* work as early as possible in the school year. The increased reading efficiency built by the program can then be put to use in all school subjects for the greater part of the school year.

Why not widely space the program practice?

Wide spacing between sessions is not recommended because the principle of reinforcement does not operate well when the program sessions are spaced far apart. When practice periods are close together, there is a carryover of learning from one day to the next. When practice periods are too far apart, there is greater risk that students will forget both the information learned and the procedures to follow. During the early stages of a learning process, practice is most efficient when closely spaced.

What about grading?

It is recommended that a student's work in the program be ungraded; the Progress Charts should tell the story. If students are reading successfully at a low level but working up to their ability, is it fair to give them a poor grade? On the other hand, such students should not be led to consider themselves above average only to find later that they are deficient in academic ability. If a grade is necessary, a dual grading system might be used—one grade for effort and another for realistic ranking of functional ability. Such a system might prove useful not only for below-grade-level students but also for above-grade-level students who do only average work because of lack of effort.

What determines the difficulty of the color levels?

A Lexile® range has been assigned to each color level, with the Lexile® range increasing for each subsequent color. An official Lexile® score has been assigned to each reading passage. Then the reading passage has been placed in the color level based on the Lexile® score. In addition, the length of the reading selections increases at every level, and the comprehension checks and word study exercises become more mechanically complex and demand increasingly sophisticated kinds of thinking.

See the chart below for the reading level and Lexile® range for each color level.

COLOR LEVELS	APPROXIMATE READING LEVEL	LEXILE RANGE
Red	1.4	240L–290L
Orange	1.6	290L–340L
Gold	1.8	340L–390L
Brown	2.0	390L–440L
Tan	2.2	440L–490L
Lime	2.4	490L–540L
Green	2.6	540L–590L
Olive	2.8	590L–640L
Aqua	3.0	640L–690L
Blue	3.5	690L–740L
Purple	4.0	740L–790L
Violet	4.5	790L–840L

34

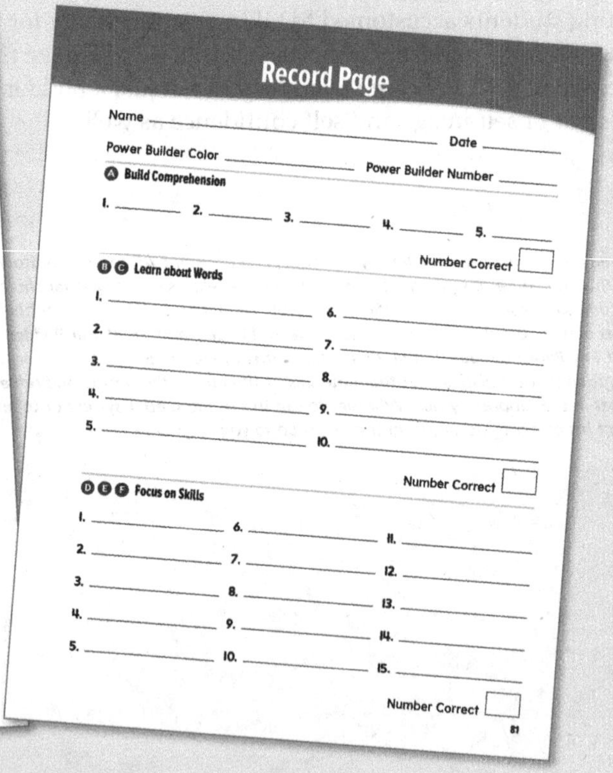

Record Page

Name ______ Date ______

Power Builder Color ______ Power Builder Number ______

A Build Comprehension

1. ___ 2. ___ 3. ___ 4. ___ 5. ___

Number Correct ☐

B C Learn about Words

1. ___ 2. ___ 3. ___ 4. ___ 5. ___ 6. ___ 7. ___ 8. ___ 9. ___ 10. ___

Number Correct ☐

D E F Focus on Skills

1. ___ 2. ___ 3. ___ 4. ___ 5. ___ 6. ___ 7. ___ 8. ___ 9. ___ 10. ___ 11. ___ 12. ___ 13. ___ 14. ___ 15. ___

Number Correct ☐

81

Power Builders

This is the core component of *SRA Reading Laboratory.* The 144 four-page *Power Builders* are arranged in color-coded levels of graduated difficulty. Each *Power Builder* has four parts:

1. High-interest fiction or nonfiction reading selection that includes engaging illustrations or photographs
2. Build Comprehension section that contains multileveled questions about the reading selection
3. Learn about Words section that includes exercises on vocabulary and word-study skills
4. Focus on Skills section that contains a variety of language, reasoning, and comprehension activities

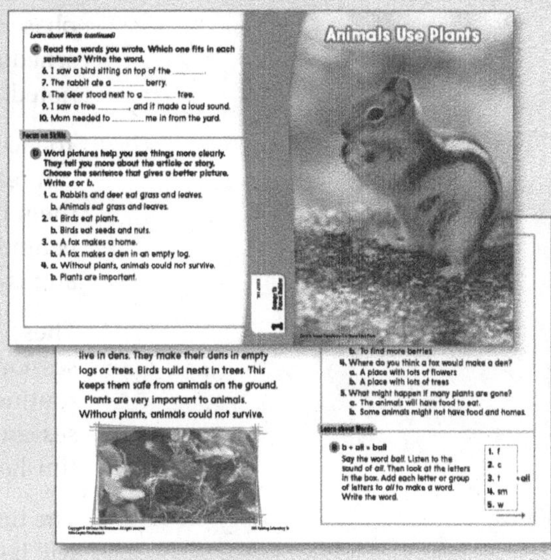

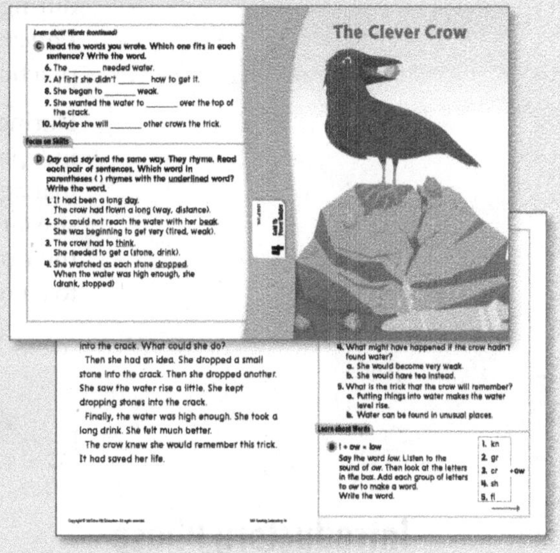

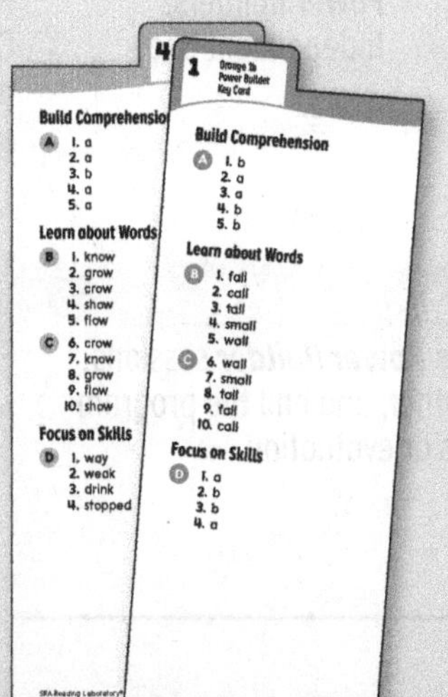

Power Builder Key Cards

Every *Power Builder* has a corresponding *Key Card* with the answers to the *Power Builder* questions. Students use the *Key Card* to score their own work.

Recommended Schedule and Teaching Plans

The following schedule covers a training phase and an independent phase for using the program materials. It is considered best to schedule the *Power Builder* sessions close together. Unless otherwise noted, each session is assumed to be twenty to forty minutes long.

To facilitate instruction, the teaching plans are "scripted" so that you can read them aloud directly to the class if you wish (or paraphrase them if you prefer). These instructions are signaled by shading behind the text. The remaining instruction is for your information and is not meant to be read aloud.

These teaching plans are fully detailed through the first seven sessions. By then the normal laboratory procedures will have become routine, and students will be working independently. The eighth session is also detailed, but it should take place when the class has finished working through the *Power Builders* for the year.

The time of your heaviest involvement in ***SRA Reading Laboratory*** will be the first seven sessions—the introductory training phase during which you will establish students' starting levels, present the ***Power Builder*** component to them, and give them opportunities to practice the basic procedures.

During the remainder of the program, students will be working independently for the most part. Your role will be primarily that of a manager/consultant who sets the times for ***SRA Reading Laboratory*** sessions and holds conferences with individual students to review their progress and help them decide whether they are ready to move to a new level.

Recommended Teaching Schedule

Introductory Phase

SESSION 1	SESSION 2	SESSION 3	SESSION 4	SESSION 5
Student Placement: Starter Stories *Page 13*	Reading Laboratory Introduction *Page 18*	Power Builder Procedures *Page 20*	Power Builders: Independent Use *Page 22*	Power Builders: Comprehension and SQR Formula *Page 25*

SESSION 6	SESSION 7	INDEPENDENT PHASE	SESSION 8
Power Builders: More Comprehension Strategies *Page 27*	Power Builders: Individual Conferences *Page 29*	Follow up with more ***Power Builder*** sessions, spaced closely together, and end the program with a final analysis or evaluation.	Final Evaluation *Page 33*

Student Placement: Starter Stories

SESSION 1

Summary: Today you will begin conducting small-group Starter Sessions using the Starter Stories from the Student Resources section of this Handbook. The six Starter Stories are used to determine the color level at which each student should enter the *Power Builder* component. The Starter Stories also give students a first taste of what it is like to read a *Power Builder* story and answer the associated questions. Depending on your class size and schedule, these Starter Sessions may take up to two weeks to complete.

Procedures

Starter Sessions are best conducted with small groups of students (no more than nine at a time) so that you can observe each student's performance and offer help as appropriate.

The most convenient sequence is to take one group through Session 1, providing complete support, then another group, then another, until all students who are ready have been through Session 1. Then you will take each group through Session 2, and so on.

Make copies of the first Starter Story on pages 57–60 and the Record Page on page 81. Distribute the copies to each student.

Read aloud or paraphrase the instructions in the shaded boxes.

> **THIS** is a *Power Builder Starter Story*. By finding out how well each of you reads, we'll decide the best place for each of you to start becoming an even better reader. How do we do this? We work together to read some Starter Stories and answer questions about them. Today we will read Starter 1.
>
> Look at the title and the cover of the story.

Teach Starter 1 as you would teach any group reading lesson. Have the group discuss the pictures. Let them relate individual experiences that come to mind. Put less-familiar words on the board, and have students pronounce them and discuss their meanings. Ask students what they think the story is about and what they may find out when they read it. Then read the story aloud to them, and discuss it briefly to make sure they understand it. Next give them time to read the story silently to themselves.*

NOW you are going to answer some questions about the story we just read. Look at the Record Page. First write your name and today's date at the top of the page. You will always write your answers on a Record Page like this one. Never write on a ***Power Builder*** because other students will use it after you. Now turn back to the story and look at the page with the questions.

Read the directions for Section A, Build Comprehension. Answer any questions students have.

WRITE your answer to each question on the lines on the Record Page. For example, the answer to Question 1 is *a* or *b*. So you will choose the letter you think is correct and write that letter on the first line. What do you think is the answer to Question 1? Yes, it's *a, how a tree is home to animals.* Write *a* on the first line next to Number 1. If you don't know an answer as you are working with the Starters or with the ***Power Builders*** on your own, just draw a circle in the blank on your Record Page.

For this Starter, ask and answer every question as a group. When Section A is completed, have students look at Section B, Learn about Words. Point out the line next to the letter *B*, and read the segmented word and then the blended word aloud. Read the directions, and answer any questions.

LOOK at the letter next to the number 1. What word do you make when you add *m* to *ad?* Yes, *mad.* Write *mad* in the blank next to 1 in the Learn about Words section on your Record Page.

****By approaching the story in this way, you have led students through a simplified version of the Survey-Question-Read (SQR) method of approaching written material. If at a later time you want to describe the method explicitly so students can consciously practice the technique in their independent work, follow the procedure detailed in Session 5 on pages 25-26.***

Continue with the remaining items, reading each new blended word with the whole group. Then read the directions for Section C, and answer any questions that students may have. Next read aloud the first sentence in this section.

LOOK at the words you wrote in Learn about Words on the Record Page. Which of those words makes sense in the sentence I just read? (*Reread the sentence.*) Yes, the best word is *had; The hill had an old tree on it.* Write *had* in the blank next to 4 in Section C.

After working through all the items in Section C, read the directions for Section D, Focus on Skills.

READ along as I read the first item aloud. Then tell me whether the sentence tells why birds live in trees. (*Read Item 1 aloud.*) Does that sentence tell why birds live in trees? Yes, so write *Yes* in the blank next to 1 in Section D on the Record Page.

When you have worked through all the items in Section D and students have written their answers to the exercises, point out that there are some leftover blanks on the Record Page. Tell them not to worry about those. Some levels of the ***Power Builders*** have enough questions to fill every blank on the Record Page.

Copy the Starter Answer Key on page 94 for each student to check his or her responses. Show them how the numbers on the Starter Answer Key correspond to the numbers on their Record Page. Demonstrate the techniques of circling each wrong answer and writing the correct response next to the error.

Record each student's progress on the Reading Progress Chart for Orange. Write *S-1* to represent *Starter 1* in the box for the ***Power Builder*** number. Use a pencil to fill in each correct answer in each section.

My Reading Progress Chart: Orange Level

Fill in the box for each correct answer on your Power Builder.

Power Builder Number	Date	A Build Comprehension	B C Learn about Words	D Focus on Skills
S-1	Oct. 12	1 2 3 4 5	1 2 3 4 5 6 7 8 9 10	1 2 3 4
		1 2 3 4 5	1 2 3 4 5 6 7 8 9 10	1 2 3 4
		1 2 3 4 5	1 2 3 4 5 6 7 8 9 10	1 2 3 4
		1 2 3 4 5	1 2 3 4 5 6 7 8 9 10	1 2 3 4

Placement Chart

Each student's starting level should be the highest level at which he or she can successfully read the selection, complete the exercises independently, and follow through accurately on procedures. As each student reaches his or her frustration level, as described below, the student will leave the Starter group and begin working independently one level lower than the Starter Story that is causing problems. General rules for determining frustration level are as follows:

- The student needs to be told as many as one-tenth of the words.
- The student scores lower than eighty percent on the exercises.
- The student relies heavily on the teacher for directions.
- The student takes an inordinate amount of time to finish.

As students continue through the Starter Stories, use the following chart to determine each student's starting level.

Placement Chart for Reading Laboratory 1b

Frustration Level	Beginning Power Builder Level
Starters 1 and 2 (Orange Level)	Red Level (Lexile® 240L–290L)
Starter 3 (Gold Level)	Orange Level (Lexile® 290L–340L)
Starter 4 (Brown Level)	Gold Level (Lexile® 340L–390L)
Starter 5 (Tan Level)	Brown Level (Lexile® 390L–440L)
Starter 6 (Green Level)	Lime Level (Lexile® 490L–540L)
All Starters read with ease	Green Level (Lexile® 540L–590L)

When students work through Starter 2, you should again supervise and provide complete support. Make sure students complete each Starter before checking their answers. As they work through Starter 3, help those who are still unsure of procedures, but allow each student to work as independently as possible. Tell them you want to see how well they remember what to do. Make sure students understand that they should look back at the story if they don't remember the answers. Remind them to put a circle in the blank and go on if they still can't find the answer.

In the coming days, continue through all six Starter Stories, encouraging greater independence with each Starter. As soon as a student's level is established, move the student into the ***Power Builder*** according to the Placement Chart guidelines. Note that Starters 1 and 2 correspond to the Orange level of ***Power Builders;*** Starters 3, 4, 5, and 6 correspond to Gold, Brown, Tan, and Green, respectively.*

As groups of students complete the Starter Stories, move on to Session 2 with them.

If a student's Lexile® level is already known, you may place the student in the level that corresponds to his or her Lexile® level. If you question the student's Lexile® level, you can use the Starter Stories to confirm the placement level.

Reading Laboratory Introduction

SESSION 2

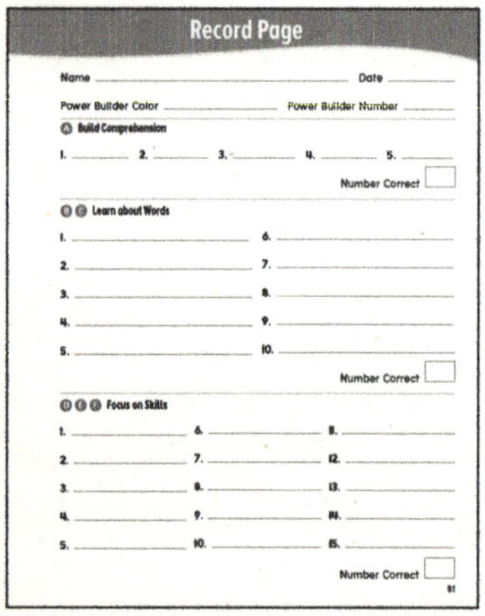

Record Page

Name ______ Date ______

Power Builder Color ______ Power Builder Number ______

A Build Comprehension

1. ______ 2. ______ 3. ______ 4. ______ 5. ______

Number Correct ☐

B C Learn about Words

1. ______ 6. ______
2. ______ 7. ______
3. ______ 8. ______
4. ______ 9. ______
5. ______ 10. ______

Number Correct ☐

D E F Focus on Skills

1. ______ 6. ______ 11. ______
2. ______ 7. ______ 12. ______
3. ______ 8. ______ 13. ______
4. ______ 9. ______ 14. ______
5. ______ 10. ______ 15. ______

Number Correct ☐

81

Summary: Today you will introduce *SRA Reading Laboratory* to students and acquaint them with the components of the program.

Procedures

Talk with students about the results of the Starter Stories they completed. Explain that there are various reading levels in the class. Hold up the Red 7 *Power Builder.*

THIS is a *Power Builder,* and it's just like the Starter Stories. First it has an interesting story. Then it has questions like the ones you answered for the Starter Stories.

The 144 *Power Builders* are grouped according to color. This *Power Builder* is story 7 from the Red level. [Point to the red color and the number 7 on the *Power Builder.*] One of these colors will be just right for you as you start out–not too easy and not too hard. When you have material that is just right for you, you can read more easily. I'll tell each of you what color you should start with, based on your work in the Starter Stories. Later you will move to other colors.

Make a copy of the Record Page from page 81 and hold it up.

THIS is a *Power Builder* Record Page. You will write all your answers to the *Power Builder* questions on a Record Page. You must never write on a *Power Builder* because other students will use it after you.

Hold up the Red 7 ***Power Builder Key Card.***

THIS is a ***Power Builder Key Card.*** When you read the Starter Stories, you used the Starter Answer Key to check your answers. Just as the Starter Answer Key has the answers to the questions for the Starter Story, a ***Power Builder Key Card*** has the answers to the questions for a ***Power Builder.***

[Point to the red color and the number 7 on the ***Key Card.]*** Each ***Power Builder*** has its own ***Key Card.*** This is the ***Key Card*** for the Red 7 ***Power Builder.*** Look at the red color. It corresponds to the red color on the ***Power Builder.*** Now look at the number 7. This is the same number as the ***Power Builder.*** The color and the number of the ***Key Card*** should always match the color and the number of the ***Power Builder.*** This is how you can tell that you are using the correct ***Key Card.***

You will check your answers using the ***Key Card.*** If you find you've made a mistake, you should always look back at the ***Power Builder*** to see where you have misunderstood. If you have trouble understanding or agreeing with an answer on the ***Key Card,*** feel free to discuss it with me.

Explain that in the next session students will work through a ***Power Builder*** and learn how to keep a record of their work.

Power Builder Procedures

SESSION 3

Summary: Today you will work with students individually or in groups of no more than three or four so they can learn the *Power Builder* procedures. If students are working in groups, make sure all students are working in the same color. You will also show students how to check and record their progress.

Procedures

Before the session, choose a *Power Builder* for each student based on his or her assigned color level. Make a copy of the Record Page and the Progress Chart for the appropriate *Power Builder* level for each student. Distribute the chosen *Power Builder* and the copies to each student.

YOU have been reading Starter Stories and answering the questions. You have learned how to record your answers on a Record Page. Today we will work through a *Power Builder* together to see how you will follow a similar procedure with the *Power Builders.* Ordinarily you will each work independently with your *Power Builders,* but today I will lead you through the process.

TIP: For organization, have students record their answers in a notebook or have a designated folder for each student to keep track of his or her Record Pages and Progress Charts.

Have students read their *Power Builders* silently. Then instruct students to write their names and the date in the spaces at the top of the Record Page.

REMEMBER that you will always write your answers on pages like this one. Never write on a *Power Builder.*

The next space is for the *Power Builder* color. There you will write the name of the color level in which you are working. After that there is a space for you to write the number that is on your *Power Builder.*

Make sure students know where to find the color and number of their *Power Builders* and where to fill in this information on the Record Page.

AFTER reading the selection in the *Power Builder,* there are questions similar to the ones you answered in the Starter Stories. Let's look at those questions. They begin with the heading *Build Comprehension.* Now silently read those questions and write the answers to those questions on your Record Sheet. You may refer back to the story if you are unsure of an answer.

Allow students to continue with the other sections of their ***Power Builders.*** Observe students' work to be sure they are writing their answers in the correct places on the Record Page.

When students have finished recording their answers, show them a ***Power Builder Key Card.***

WHEN you finish a ***Power Builder,*** you will find the ***Key Card*** whose color and number match the ***Power Builder*** you read. You will use the ***Key Card*** to check your answers. If you have a different answer from an answer on the ***Key Card,*** you should draw a circle around your answer and write the correct answer next to it.

Remind students that it is okay to get answers wrong. The questions are not for a grade, but for accurate placement to increase learning.

Give students enough time to check their answers and mark any incorrect answers.

NOW find the heading on your Record Page that says *Build Comprehension.* Look at your answers in the blanks below the heading. Find the box that says *Number Correct.* Count the number of your correct answers. Remember, if you have any answers that are circled, they are to be counted as incorrect answers. Write the number of correct answers in the box. Then do the same thing for the Learn about Words and Focus on Skills exercises.

When students have finished scoring their work, have them look at their Progress Chart.

GO to the first line on the Progress Chart, and write in the number of the ***Power Builder*** you just completed. Then write today's date. Finally use your pencil to fill in the number of each answer you got correct in each section of the ***Power Builder.***

Power Builders: Independent Use

SESSION 4

Summary: Today students will begin working with *Power Builders* independently at their own pace. First, however, you may want to review the *Power Builder* procedures with students. Keep in mind that students may not be able to work entirely independently at this stage. You will probably need to be available to answer a number of questions and assist with procedures.

It is important to answer questions and give help promptly at the moment of need. Students can then quickly move ahead on their own. A major advantage of ***SRA Reading Laboratory*** is that it is student directed and it frees the teacher to give prompt help whenever it is needed.

Encourage students to take responsibility and pride in their independent work and progress.

In general allow approximately twenty to forty minutes for each session with the ***Power Builders.*** Due to individual differences, students will work at different speeds. Early in the program, some students may require more time to complete a ***Power Builder.*** Later in the program, some students will finish their work early. However, these students should not begin another ***Power Builder.*** If work is hurried, a student's work may degenerate into a pointless race with time. If students have time remaining, allow them to do an activity that is a change of pace. For example, you could allow them to read library books or other materials for pleasure.

Procedures

Before the session begins, you will need to decide the general procedure for using ***Power Builders*** in your classroom. You can either have students select their own ***Power Builders*** individually, or you may want to appoint group leaders in charge of selecting the ***Power Builders*** and handing them out.*

Next choose a ***Power Builder*** for each student based on his or her assigned color level. Make a copy of the Record Page and the Progress Chart for the appropriate ***Power Builder*** level for each student. Distribute the chosen ***Power Builder*** and the copies to each student.

***You should establish goals that work for your class. Individual student choice encourages personal responsibility. Assigning group leaders and rotating leadership roles fosters a team approach and encourages leadership skills.*

THIS is the color in which you will start your ***Power Builder*** work. This color was chosen based on the work you did with the Starter Stories. Look at the color and the number showing on your ***Power Builder.*** It is on the edge of your ***Power Builder.*** Your ***Power Builder*** must always be the color that is marked on your Progress Chart.

Look at the number of your ***Power Builder.*** Now look on the Progress Chart. Notice the "Power Builder Number" column. Write the number of your ***Power Builder*** in the first block. Then write today's date in the next column. You will do this each time you receive a new ***Power Builder.*** In this way your chart will always show which ***Power Builders*** you have already completed, so you won't repeat the same one twice.

You can read the ***Power Builders*** within your color in any order. For example, you could read Number 12 first and Number 1 last. You will need to work on ***Power Builders*** within the same color until your scores show that you are ready to move to another level. Most of the time, you will need to complete at least four ***Power Builders*** before going on to a new color. We will have conferences together to help us decide when you should move on to a new level. Remember, your work is not a race. Work at the right pace for you to improve your reading skills. This will be different for everyone.

Have students look at the Record Page.

AFTER you have read the ***Power Builder*** selection, you will use a Record Page to write your answers to the questions. Next you will check your answers against the ***Power Builder Key Card*** that has the same color and number as those on your ***Power Builder.***

Consider having a conference with your students after they complete four stories to see if they are ready to move to the next level.

Encourage students to use their Progress Charts during parent-teacher meetings. Students can explain to their parents or guardians what the Progress Chart demonstrates. This will encourage students to take ownership over their own learning.

Hold up a ***Power Builder*** and a matching ***Key Card*** from the ***Reading Laboratory*** box.

REMEMBER each ***Power Builder*** has its own ***Power Builder Key Card.*** When you finish your ***Power Builder,*** go to the ***Reading Laboratory*** box, and take the matching ***Key Card*** back to your desk. Using your Record Page and the ***Key Card,*** check your answers. On your Record Page, circle any incorrect answers, and write the correct answer next to each incorrect answer. Don't forget to write the number of correct answers in each box next to the words *Number Correct.*

Now ask students to look at their Progress Chart.

FINALLY you will need to fill the boxes on your Progress Chart. This is an important step in tracking your progress in your reading journey. Using a pencil, fill in the box for each correct answer. Now we have reviewed every step for working with the ***Power Builders.*** You are ready to start working with the ***Power Builders*** on your own. Ask me at any time if you are not sure what to do next.

Have students begin their ***Power Builders.***

SESSION 5

Summary: Today you will conduct a Comprehension Strategy Lesson with small groups of students before they work through a *Power Builder* on their own. This is the first of two lessons designed to introduce comprehension strategies and metacognitive techniques that will help students get the most from their reading.

Procedures

Hold up *Power Builder* Red-5, *Dee's Trees.*

WHEN you read a story, you read sentences that belong together. They all help to tell about one main idea. The main idea is what the story is mostly about. Clues about the main idea will help you understand what you read.

Suppose you saw the question *What is the main idea of this story?* What would you look for in the story in order to choose the correct answer?

Hold up the *Power Builder* again and point to each element as you discuss the following list.

Here are some things to do:

- Look at the picture on the cover.
- Read the title.
- Read the first sentence.
- Read the last paragraph.

All these items are clues that will help you find the story's main idea. What do you think the story on this *Power Builder* might be about? How would you answer the question *What is the main idea?*

Accept any reasonable answers that students can justify as a description of the main idea. If a response deals with something that seems unreasonable or illogical, ask the student who offered the response to tell which clues he or she used to find that main idea.

I KNOW you probably want to read the story now to find out whether we were correct about the main idea, but we aren't going to read it today. Why do you suppose it's important to know the main idea of a story before you start to read it? If you have an idea of what the story is about and what you might expect to find out from it, you think about what you're reading, and you understand it better. You might not always want to read the last paragraph because sometimes knowing the ending spoils the surprise of the story. However, looking at the title, studying the picture, and reading the first sentence before you start reading the story are good ways to get ready to understand what you'll be reading.

Next write the word *Survey* on the board, using an oversized *S.*

THIS word is *Survey.* It means "to look over." You have just been surveying a story. Did you think of any questions as you were surveying the story?

When some students have responded, write the word *Question* with an oversized *Q* under the word *Survey.* Under the word *Question,* write the word *Read* with an oversized *R.*

IF you remember SQR, it will help you read and study better. First you survey, then you question, and then you are ready to read. Now let's review what we've learned today.

Conduct a brief review of the four strategies for finding the main idea, as well as the SQR formula.

THESE are steps you can use to help you understand anything you read. Try to remember these steps when you read your ***Power Builders*** and anything else you read on your own.

Allow students to work independently on their ***Power Builders.***

Power Builders: More Comprehension Strategies

SESSION 6

Summary: Today you will conduct the second Comprehension Strategy Lesson with students.

Procedures

Hold up ***Power Builder*** Red-5 and ask students to look at the title *Dee's Trees*. Then point out the story on the inside of the ***Power Builder***. Remind students that recently they looked at the title, studied the picture, read the first sentence, and read the last paragraph of the story to find the main idea. Call on volunteers to recall their predictions about the story's main idea.

> **KNOWING** the main idea will help you understand what you're reading, but you'll understand it even better if you keep asking yourself questions as you read. In this lesson, we are going to read the story and ask ourselves some questions.

Read aloud the first paragraph of *Dee's Trees*.

> **ASK** yourself the following questions to check your thoughts on the main idea. *What did I think the story might be about? What do I know now? Was I correct?*

Confirm students' earlier predictions about the story. Then read aloud the second paragraph of the story.

> **NOW** ask yourself the following question: *Do I understand what I just read in this paragraph?* Tell me in your own words what we just read.

Students' responses will probably be worded much like the original paragraph. Accept any answers that show an understanding of events in that paragraph.

Before You Read

Use your eyes to get clues about the main idea:

- Look at the picture.
- Read the title.
- Read the first sentence.
- Read the last paragraph.

As You Read

Ask yourself these questions to make sure you understand:

- Was I correct about what the story is mostly about?
- Do I understand what I just read?
- What did I learn from this story?

IF you didn't understand what you read, it would be a good idea to read that paragraph again.

Read aloud the last paragraph of the story.

NOW we have read the whole story. Ask yourself one last question: *What did I learn from this story?*

Allow students to discuss any aspects of the story that interest them.

As you read a story, ask yourselves the questions we just discussed. These questions will help you get the most out of what you read.

After you read a story, you usually know more than you did before. There are many ways to find out how well you understood what you read. One simple way is to answer questions.

When you are working with the ***Power Builders***, you will read the story and answer questions to check your understanding. You will write your answers on a Record Page, not on the ***Power Builder***. Remember, you can always turn back to the story if you need help.

If you follow the steps we've talked about, you will probably find it easier to understand and remember what you read.

You may want to display the questions on a board or wall for students to refer to as they read the ***Power Builders.***

Power Builders: Individual Conferences

SESSION 7

Summary: Today you'll review the work individual students have been doing. One of the first things you want to find out is whether each student has been placed in the correct color and corresponding Lexile® level in ***SRA Reading Laboratory.*** The Starter Stories you administered earlier are not precise instruments, although they are a good general indicator of the best level at which a student should begin. Psychological factors, some uneasiness about working under pressure of time, or simply lucky guessing may result in better or worse performance with the Starter Stories than actual ability warrants. If this was the case, it should become apparent now as you review the student's Progress Charts, and an adjustment of the student's placement can be made.

Procedures

Once the ***Power Builder*** procedures are established, you will hold a counseling session with each student. While the class is working with ***Power Builders*** or doing free reading, begin conferences with individual students. Ask a student to come to your desk, bringing along his or her latest Progress Chart. Begin by asking the student how he or she is doing and how he or she is enjoying the work. Then examine the Progress Chart. If you have any questions about how accurately the chart reflects the student's true abilities, he or she should read to you from one of the ***Power Builders*** so you can make a more direct assessment.

To the greatest extent possible, your student conferences should be cooperative ventures in which you and the student reach a decision together regarding the student's performance. The student should be encouraged to help decide whether he or she is ready to advance to a new level, or whether remaining in the current level for a while longer is appropriate. Students unused to having such responsibility for their own instruction and progress will probably be a little hesitant to join in the decision at first. Soon, however, they will become accustomed to the idea and will acquire considerable skill in analyzing their work.

In these conferences, students may reveal certain concerns. They may feel ashamed to make mistakes. If so, explain that it is natural to make mistakes and that mistakes can help you learn, provided you take the time to find out why you made the mistake.

Students may be worried because of the irregular appearance–highs and lows–of their Progress Charts. Explain that there is no perfect progress from day to day. The important thing is the general direction in which they are moving.

Individual development and progress is the goal.

Students may be worried about competition with others. Emphasize that students develop at different rates. The important thing is each student's development. Students who advance through the lower levels make as much progress as those who advance through the higher levels.

Advancing to a Higher Color Level

It is during these student conferences that you will consider whether students are ready to move to a higher color level. During the program, some students can be expected to advance three, four, or even five color levels.

Generally, a typical student should complete four to six *Power Builders* and achieve scores of eighty percent or higher in both the Build Comprehension and the Learn about Words sections before moving to a higher color level. Some students may need to finish all the *Power Builders* before moving to a new color level.

Occasionally, students will not want to advance because they enjoy the success they are having with the easier work. Then you will have to prod them a little. On the other hand, there are always a few students who are too anxious to advance. You will tactfully have to slow their progress without destroying their enthusiasm. In either case, the Progress Charts are the basis for wise decisions.

Interpreting Progress Charts

If a student is not moving smoothly through a color level–improving scores steadily–review the Progress Charts with the Comprehension and Word-Study Skills Chart for that color level. On the next page is a sample of a typical Progress Chart. A study of this chart will help you guide students in evaluating their own work and programming their own learning.

1 The student has been working at the Orange Level. Her Progress Chart shows that she has read Orange ***Power Builders*** 12, 3, 4, 9, and 1.

2 Look at the Build Comprehension section on the sample Progress Chart. You see that only in ***Power Builder*** 3 has she scored below eighty percent. She missed Questions 2 and 5, which involve identifying literary elements according to the sample Orange Level Comprehension and Word-Study Skills Chart.

The Comprehension and Word-Study Skills Chart shows that ***Power Builders*** 7, 10, 11, and 12 will give the student further practice in identifying literary elements.

3 You also notice that the student has had difficulty with Learn about Words. Her Record Pages show that her problem lies in Section C, using words in context. ***Power Builders*** 7, 10, 11, and 12 will not only help her with identifying literary elements (Section A) but will give her practice in using words.

4 Naturally, you will not simply assign additional ***Power Builders;*** you will want to model and reteach as necessary. You will want to discuss all problem areas with the students. You may find that low scores in a particular section are a matter of having misunderstood the directions for that section. Remind students to look back at incorrect answers to see why they missed them and to discuss them with you if they still don't understand.

Use the Progress Charts to help you differentiate instruction if needed.

My Reading Progress Chart: Orange Level

Fill in the box for each correct answer on your Power Builder.

Power Builder Number	Date	A Build Comprehension	B C Learn about Words	D Focus on Skills
12	Oct. 9	1 2 3 4 5	1 2 3 4 5 6 7 8 9 10	1 2 3 4
3	Oct. 11	1 2 3 4 5	1 2 3 4 5 6 7 8 9 10	1 2 3 4
4	Oct. 13	1 2 3 4 5	1 2 3 4 5 6 7 8 9 10	1 2 3 4
9	Oct. 16	1 2 3 4 5	1 2 3 4 5 6 7 8 9 10	1 2 3 4
1	Oct. 19	1 2 3 4 5	1 2 3 4 5 6 7 8 9 10	1 2 3 4
		1 2 3 4 5	1 2 3 4 5 6 7 8 9 10	1 2 3 4
		1 2 3 4 5	1 2 3 4 5 6 7 8 9 10	1 2 3 4
		1 2 3 4 5	1 2 3 4 5 6 7 8 9 10	1 2 3 4
		1 2 3 4 5	1 2 3 4 5 6 7 8 9 10	1 2 3 4
		1 2 3 4 5	1 2 3 4 5 6 7 8 9 10	1 2 3 4
		1 2 3 4 5	1 2 3 4 5 6 7 8 9 10	1 2 3 4
		1 2 3 4 5	1 2 3 4 5 6 7 8 9 10	1 2 3 4

Orange	Power Builder Number											
	1	2	3	4	5	6	7	8	9	10	11	12
A Build Comprehension	Item Numbers											
Identifying the Main Idea	1	1	1	1	1	1	1	1	1	1	1	1
Drawing Conclusions	2, 3			4		5	2, 3, 4	3, 5	4, 5	4, 5	2, 5	
Making Inferences	4				3, 4			2, 4		3	4	2
Understanding Cause and Effect		2, 3, 4	4		2	2						4
Sequence		5				3, 4			2			
Predicting Outcomes	5				5							
Identifying Literary Elements			2, 3, 5				5			2	3	3
Recognizing Problems and Solutions				2, 3, 5					3			5
Learn about Words												
B Minimal-Contrast Word Building	all	ad	ad	ight	ake	ay	ight	et	ake	ell	ot	at
C Using Words in Context	●	●	●	●	●	●	●	●	●	●	●	●
Focus on Skills												
Descriptive Language	D							D			D	
Real or Make-Believe			D		D							D
Antonyms		D				D			D			
Alphabetical Order				D			D			D		

Final Evaluation

SESSION 8

Summary: When your class has finished *Power Builders* for the year, lead a class discussion of what they have learned about reading and what they have enjoyed about *SRA Reading Laboratory.* Paying careful attention to students' comments can help you identify ways to work more effectively with individuals and the class as a whole.

Procedures

Encourage students to tell a little about their favorite story or to tell something new and interesting they learned from reading the *Power Builders.* Make sure each student who wants to share something has a chance to do so.

Review the comprehension strategy lessons. Ask students how they have used the strategies in their other classwork. Ask them to share any other ways in which their *Power Builder* work has helped with other reading they have done.

Remind students to continue using the techniques and strategies they have learned as they read, both for reading textbooks and for pleasure reading.

Encourage students to apply the strategies they have learned in their other classwork.

APPENDIX A: Answers to Frequently Asked Questions

When should SRA Reading Laboratory *be started?*

Teachers generally find it most desirable to schedule *SRA Reading Laboratory* work as early as possible in the school year. The increased reading efficiency built by the program can then be put to use in all school subjects for the greater part of the school year.

Why not widely space the program practice?

Wide spacing between sessions is not recommended because the principle of reinforcement does not operate well when the program sessions are spaced far apart. When practice periods are close together, there is a carryover of learning from one day to the next. When practice periods are too far apart, there is greater risk that students will forget both the information learned and the procedures to follow. During the early stages of a learning process, practice is most efficient when closely spaced.

What about grading?

It is recommended that a student's work in the program be ungraded; the Progress Charts should tell the story. If students are reading successfully at a low level but working up to their ability, is it fair to give them a poor grade? On the other hand, such students should not be led to consider themselves above average only to find later that they are deficient in academic ability. If a grade is necessary, a dual grading system might be used–one grade for effort and another for realistic ranking of functional ability. Such a system might prove useful not only for below-grade-level students but also for above-grade-level students who do only average work because of lack of effort.

What determines the difficulty of the color levels?

A Lexile® range has been assigned to each color level, with the Lexile® range increasing for each subsequent color. An official Lexile® score has been assigned to each reading passage. Then the reading passage has been placed in the appropriate color level based on the Lexile® score. In addition, the length of the reading selections increases at every level, and the comprehension checks and word study exercises become more mechanically complex and demand increasingly sophisticated kinds of thinking.

See the chart below for the reading level and Lexile® range for each color level in the 1b *SRA Reading Laboratory.*

COLOR LEVEL	APPROXIMATE READING LEVEL	LEXILE® RANGE
Red	1.4	240L–290L
Orange	1.6	290L–340L
Gold	1.8	340L–390L
Brown	2.0	390L–440L
Tan	2.2	440L–490L
Lime	2.4	490L–540L
Green	2.6	540L–590L
Olive	2.8	590L–640L
Aqua	3.0	640L–690L
Blue	3.5	690L–740L
Purple	4.0	740L–790L
Violet	4.5	790L–840L

What about competition and cheating?

Competition and cheating are closely interrelated problems. If a student takes advantage of the ***Key Cards'*** availability to copy answers or if the student otherwise falsifies his or her scores, it is probably done in an effort to keep up with other class members or to get ahead of them.

For this reason, it is important in the initial stages of the program to convey the idea that multilevel work does not involve a race among classmates–that different students will be in different color levels because students differ, and this program provides materials that are appropriate for each one.

It is also important to minimize the idea that moving from one color level to another is the badge of success. This is *one kind* of success, which might be called vertical progress. But there is also horizontal progress–success in each ***Power Builder*** a student completes within a level. Each ***Power Builder*** presents new skills to master or different approaches to similar skills. Students should, therefore, be encouraged to see their goal as one of simply working as well as possible with the materials that are appropriate for them. They should not view climbing up the ladder of color levels as the only goal of their work. Obviously, you must play a key role in forming appropriate attitudes about what constitutes success.

Students hurt only themselves when they seek status among classmates by defeating the program's continuous placement mechanism and by moving ahead in the color sequence by means of copied answers or falsified scores. Those students miss needed practice and encounter material that is too difficult. You can try to communicate this idea, although obviously there will be resistance if a student has been taunted by a classmate for being "only in Orange," for example. You then face the traditional problem of how to motivate a student to do what's best in the long run when the student prefers to do what seems to provide immediate status and peer acceptance. It is a problem that occurs in all areas of student behavior when a competitive atmosphere exists, and it is by no means a unique problem to this program. Teachers who have found ways to remedy this problem in other areas of school life will probably handle it successfully in connection with this program.

If cheating is apparent, a confidential talk with the student is a good idea. You can stress the idea that "one only cheats oneself" and help the student understand that hurrying from level to level is not the aim of the program. Remember, too, that by spot-checking for errors and by praising accuracy and neatness in scoring, calculating, and charting, you can set up an atmosphere that discourages cheating.

Finally, remember that it is *not* cheating for students to look back at the story in order to answer the comprehension and vocabulary checks. Indeed, looking back should be encouraged as preferable to guessing or relying on uncertain recollections. Looking back is what we all do (and *should* do) in real-life reading situations when we want to be sure about what we have read. Once this is understood, some students may no longer have the need to misuse the ***Key Card*** or alter their scores.

What about record keeping?

Because *SRA Reading Laboratory* is student directed, you enter no scores and correct no papers. Each student keeps all the necessary records on the Record Pages and the Progress Charts. The records each student maintains are invaluable guides to the diagnosis of his or her reading difficulties, progress, and long-range educational potential.

The value of these student-kept records is threefold:

(1) In parent conferences, the Progress Charts form an objective basis for interpreting school progress in the vital area of reading. They provide a direct and unbiased reflection of the student's day-to-day work.

(2) In student guidance, the Progress Charts represent a cumulative record of the student's actual *functional* ability to learn through reading. Such information is useful in helping both the parent and the teacher or guidance worker–as well as the student–in realistically planning the student's educational future.

(3) In curriculum improvement, analysis of the functional reading levels of pupils may indicate to the teacher or curriculum worker a need for revising upward or downward the difficulty level of offerings in the various subject areas. Such a study might point out a need for further steps toward individualizing learning opportunities.

APPENDIX B: Power Builder Titles

Level	Title	Word Count	LEXILE®
Red	**Lexile® Range 240L–290L**		
1	*The Lost Puppy*	73	280L
2	*A New Home*	76	280L
3	*Mr. Miller and Tiny*	84	240L
4	*Space Station Home*	75	270L
5	*Dee's Trees*	85	250L
6	*What Cookie Found*	82	280L
7	*The Race*	76	290L
8	*What a Trick!*	86	280L
9	*Little Hen Sees Something New*	85	260L
10	*Marty's Picture*	85	270L
11	*Noises in the Night*	89	280L
12	*The Picnic*	82	270L
Orange	**Lexile® Range 290L–340L**		
1	*Animals Use Plants*	95	310L
2	*A Mouse in the Royal Kitchen*	111	340L
3	*Who Did It?*	107	300L
4	*The Flying Saucer*	109	300L
5	*Stone Soup*	104	340L
6	*A New Friend*	111	310L
7	*The Zoo Doctor*	112	330L
8	*Raindrop*	113	330L
9	*Gold for a Night's Sleep*	124	320L
10	*Flying High*	109	320L
11	*The Lion and the Mouse*	108	340L
12	*A Snowy Surprise*	92	340L

Level	Title	Word Count	LEXILE®
Gold	**Lexile® Range 340L–390L**		
1	*Deanna's Surprise*	126	360L
2	*Monkey Keeps Quiet*	129	370L
3	*Dogs*	125	380L
4	*The Clever Crow*	131	350L
5	*Beth's First Swim Meet*	143	390L
6	*The Picture*	120	390L
7	*The Golden Touch*	140	390L
8	*Hard Times*	140	390L
9	*Wishing*	133	370L
10	*The Echo*	131	370L
11	*I See You!*	150	340L
12	*What Is It?*	137	360L
Brown	**Lexile® Range 390L–440L**		
1	*The Bamboo Basket*	191	410L
2	*The Camping Trip*	163	410L
3	*What Do Living Things Need?*	148	430L
4	*Tony's Pets*	174	400L
5	*Moving Day*	176	420L
6	*Visiting Mars*	147	430L
7	*The Parrot and the Plumber*	175	410L
8	*Remembering*	160	430L
9	*The Meeting*	158	400L
10	*Food for Winter*	158	390L
11	*Changing Rocks*	147	410L
12	*The Lost Jacket*	166	400L

Level	Title	Word Count	LEXILE®
Tan	**Lexile® Range 440L–490L**		
1	*Stories in the Sky*	189	470L
2	*The Singing Whales*	200	450L
3	*Mushroom Mine*	193	490L
4	*Into the Deep*	210	490L
5	*The Blue Ridge Mountains*	193	460L
6	*A Special Gift*	187	450L
7	*Auntie Elephant*	166	480L
8	*I Can Do That!*	211	440L
9	*The Wrinkled Grape*	185	450L
10	*The Choice*	196	440L
11	*Land of Bikes*	186	490L
12	*Our Map of the Ocean*	192	470L
Lime	**Lexile® Range 490L–540L**		
1	*The Surprised Knight*	220	500L
2	*Madurodam: The Netherlands' Toy Town*	216	500L
3	*Hamm and Sid's New Home*	231	540L
4	*Who Uses Tools?*	195	520L
5	*The Snowstorm*	243	500L
6	*Dancers in the Wild*	224	500L
7	*A Stick Will Do the Trick*	246	500L
8	*Animals in Stories*	215	540L
9	*The Buried Town*	228	520L
10	*Will You Ever See a Wombat?*	246	530L
11	*Silly Sunny!*	252	510L
12	*When the Robin Goes Bobbin'*	235	520L

Appendix B

Level	Title	Word Count	LEXILE®
Green	**Lexile® Range 540L–590L**		
1	*Borrowing Burrows*	312	540L
2	*Pancake's Prize*	276	560L
3	*Charles Dickens and the Little Children*	281	590L
4	*Jackal and Lion*	283	550L
5	*You See Only Part of a Tree*	273	560L
6	*Who Chose Best*	305	560L
7	*Nellie Bly: Star Reporter*	305	590L
8	*The Perfect Gift*	251	580L
9	*Life in the Ocean*	289	550L
10	*Dribble, Shoot, Score!*	263	560L
11	*Highways in the Sky*	286	570L
12	*Glenn Cunningham: He Wouldn't Quit*	288	550L
Olive	**Lexile® Range 590L–640L**		
1	*Big Cats*	331	630L
2	*A Surprise Work of Art*	367	610L
3	*The Towers of Simon Rodia*	375	610L
4	*A Small Favor*	383	600L
5	*Sonja's First Skates*	314	620L
6	*CHIRP!*	357	610L
7	*The Gift of a Dog*	316	610L
8	*Life Cycles*	347	590L
9	*Taste Buds*	354	590L
10	*King Wohali*	411	600L
11	*Weather the Weather*	370	620L
12	*A Snowman for Moose*	345	590L

Level	Title	Word Count	LEXILE®
Aqua	**Lexile® Range 640L–690L**		
1	*The Fox and the Grapes*	395	640L
2	*Jamestown*	307	690L
3	*The Clever Giant*	427	660L
4	*Rules and Laws*	358	690L
5	*A Tricky Spider*	375	690L
6	*Rachel Carson's* Silent Spring	431	650L
7	*Hey, Peanuts!*	435	640L
8	*Star Flight*	385	640L
9	*The Problem*	430	690L
10	*Why We Have Winter*	412	690L
11	*The Apple Dumpling*	430	690L
12	*A Winter Bouquet*	445	690L
Blue	**Lexile® Range 690L–740L**		
1	*Rhyme Time*	418	700L
2	*Benjamin Franklin*	421	740L
3	*The Memory Box*	483	700L
4	*The Evidence Is In!*	404	690L
5	*The Tale of One Candle*	514	700L
6	*Kordell Solves a Problem*	500	690L
7	*Amazing Desert Animals*	407	740L
8	*Life in the Desert*	461	740L
9	*Singers of History*	406	720L
10	*Close to the Sun*	460	740L
11	*Who Is the Cleverest?*	493	690L
12	*A Gathering in the Meadow*	487	700L

Appendix B

Level	Title	Word Count	LEXILE®
Purple	**Lexile® Range 740L–790L**		
1	*Election and Voting*	436	790L
2	*A Dog Named Toad*	561	790L
3	*The Farmer*	550	780L
4	*Ocean Inhabitants*	536	790L
5	*Investigation at Yowell Creek*	592	750L
6	*Choices about Money*	471	790L
7	*Arctic Animals*	576	760L
8	*The Train*	540	750L
9	*Energy All around Us*	520	790L
10	*Little Libraries*	549	790L
11	*Regions of the United States*	473	790L
12	*William Halsted*	501	780L
Violet	**Lexile® Range 790L–840L**		
1	*Athena and Arachne*	628	810L
2	*Ancient Egypt*	674	800L
3	*One-Room Schoolhouses*	568	840L
4	*After the Hurricane*	649	800L
5	*What Does It Mean?*	573	800L
6	*Sally Ride-Space Explorer*	582	840L
7	*A Piece to Remember*	656	800L
8	*Abraham Lincoln*	646	800L
9	*Paul Bunyan and the Great Lakes*	582	830L
10	*The Monkey Whose Tail Was Not Caught*	599	790L
11	*Taking Care of Earth*	640	840L
12	*The Job of Government*	617	830L

APPENDIX C: Comprehension and Word-Study Skills Charts

Red	Power Builder Number											
	1	2	3	4	5	6	7	8	9	10	11	12
A Build Comprehension	Item Numbers											
Identifying the Main Idea	1	1	1	1	1	1	1	1	1	1	1	1
Drawing Conclusions	2	5	3	2, 3		2, 4	3, 4	4, 5	3, 4	3	2	
Making Inferences			5	4, 5				3		5	3	5
Understanding Cause and Effect						5	2, 5	2				
Comparing and Contrasting					2, 4	3					4, 5	2, 3, 4
Predicting Outcomes	5		4		5							
Identifying Literary Elements	3, 4	4	2		3				2, 5	2, 4		
Sequence		2, 3										
Learn about Words												
B Minimal-Contrast Word Building	ad	ot	ot	ad	an	at	at	ay	an	ave	ight	ay
C Using Words in Context	●	●	●	●	●	●	●	●	●	●	●	●
Focus on Skills												
Giving Reasons	D						D		D			
Rhyming Words				D	D					D		
Synonyms		D				D						D
Antonyms			D					D			D	

Orange	Power Builder Number											
	1	2	3	4	5	6	7	8	9	10	11	12
A Build Comprehension	**Item Numbers**											
Identifying the Main Idea	1	1	1	1	1	1	1	1	1	1	1	1
Drawing Conclusions	2, 3			4		5	2, 3, 4	3, 5	4, 5	4, 5	2, 5	
Making Inferences	4				3, 4			2, 4		3	4	2
Understanding Cause and Effect		2, 3, 4	4		2	2						4
Sequence		5				3, 4			2			
Predicting Outcomes	5				5							
Identifying Literary Elements			2, 3, 5				5			2	3	3
Recognizing Problems and Solutions				2, 3, 5					3			5
Learn about Words												
B Minimal-Contrast Word Building	all	ad	ad	ight	ake	ay	ight	et	ake	ell	ot	at
C Using Words in Context	●	●	●	●	●	●	●	●	●	●	●	●
Focus on Skills												
Descriptive Language	D							D			D	
Real or Make-Believe			D		D							D
Antonyms		D				D			D			
Alphabetical Order				D			D			D		

Gold	Power Builder Number											
	1	2	3	4	5	6	7	8	9	10	11	12
A Build Comprehension	Item Numbers											
Identifying the Main Idea	1	1	1	1	1	1	1	1	1	1	1	1
Drawing Conclusions		2	2, 4	5	4	2	3, 5	4, 5	4	2, 3	2	5
Making Inferences	5		3, 5	4	3			3	3	5	5	3
Understanding Cause and Effect		4		2, 3			2			4	3, 4	
Comparing and Contrasting							4					2, 4
Sequence	2, 4											
Identifying Literary Elements	3	3, 5			2, 5	3, 4		2	2, 5			
Identifying Real and Make-Believe						5						
Learn about Words												
B Minimal-Contrast Word Building	ow	all	et	ow	y	all	ot	all	et	ay	ook	ay
C Using Words in Context	●	●	●	●	●	●	●	●	●	●	●	●
Focus on Skills												
Sequence	D				D					D		
Rhyming Words				D			D		D			
Past Tense		D				D					D	
Synonyms			D					D				D

Brown	Power Builder Number											
	1	2	3	4	5	6	7	8	9	10	11	12
A Build Comprehension	**Item Numbers**											
Identifying the Main Idea	1	1	1	1	1	1	1	1	1	1	1	1
Drawing Conclusions	2	2, 3	2, 5			2, 3, 4		2	2	2	5	3, 5
Making Inferences	5			3, 4	2, 3		4	3	5			
Understanding Cause and Effect	4		3				2, 3			3, 4	4	2, 4
Comparing and Contrasting			4	2						5	2, 3	
Predicting Outcomes		4			4, 5	5		4, 5	4			
Identifying Literary Elements	3	5					5		3			
Identifying Real and Make-Believe				5								
Learn about Words												
B Minimal-Contrast Word Building	old	ight	ake	ay	et	ow	ock	ack	are	ut	ow	ock
C Using New Words in Context	●	●	●	●	●	●	●	●	●	●	●	●
Focus on Skills												
Predictions		D				D						D
Descriptive Language				D				D		D		
Contractions			D		D				D			
Punctuation	D						D				D	

Tan	Power Builder Number											
	1	2	3	4	5	6	7	8	9	10	11	12
A Build Comprehension	**Item Numbers**											
Identifying the Main Idea	1	1	1	1	1	1	1	1	1	1	1	1
Drawing Conclusions	5			2, 4	3	5	3	4	2		3	5
Making Inferences	3		4		4	2	4, 5	5	4	2	2, 4, 5	4
Understanding Cause and Effect	2		3	3			2		3			2, 3
Comparing and Contrasting		2, 3, 4	2, 5	5	2				5			
Predicting Outcomes	4	5			5	3, 4						
Identifying Literary Elements								2, 3				
Recognizing Problems and Solutions										3, 4, 5		
Learn about Words												
B Word Study												
Compound Words		●			●				●			
Regular Plurals			●				●				●	
Contractions	●							●				●
Possessives				●		●				●		
C Using New Words in Context	●	●	●	●	●	●	●	●	●	●	●	●
Focus on Skills												
Sequence				D			D				D	
Similes	D							D				D
Digraphs		D				D				D		
Pronoun Antecedents			D		D				D			

Lime	Power Builder Number											
	1	2	3	4	5	6	7	8	9	10	11	12
Ⓐ Build Comprehension	**Item Numbers**											
Identifying the Main Idea	1	1	1	1	1	1	1	1	1	1	1	1
Drawing Conclusions		2		2, 4	2	2, 4	4	3	4	3	3	2, 3, 5
Making Inferences	2		5	5	4		3		5		2	4
Understanding Cause and Effect	3		2		3	3	2	4	2	2, 4	4	
Comparing and Contrasting		5		3		5			3	5		
Predicting Outcomes	5	3, 4						2			5	
Identifying Literary Elements	4		3, 4		5		5	5				
Learn about Words												
Ⓑ Word Study												
Compound Words	●								●		●	
Regular Plurals				●		●				●		
Contractions		●			●			●				
Possessives			●				●					●
Ⓒ Using New Words in Context	●	●	●	●	●	●	●	●	●	●	●	●
Focus on Skills												
Story Map	D										E	
Descriptive Language		D			D				E			
Predictions			D				D			D		
Topic Details				D		D		D		E		
Blends	E					E						E
Pronoun Antecedents		E			E						D	
Past Tense			E				E		D			
Punctuation				E				E				D

Green	Power Builder Number											
	1	2	3	4	5	6	7	8	9	10	11	12
A Build Comprehension	Item Numbers											
Identifying the Main Idea	1	1	1	1	1	1	1	1	1	1	1	1
Drawing Conclusions	5	5		3	2, 5	2	4		4	4	3, 4	2, 5
Making Inferences		4	4	5		4, 5	3	2, 3	5	2, 3, 5		4
Understanding Cause and Effect	4	3	2, 3, 5	4		3					2	3
Comparing and Contrasting	3				3, 4				2, 3			
Predicting Outcomes	2	2						5			5	
Identifying Literary Elements				2			2, 5	4				
Learn about Words												
B Word Meaning in Context	●	●	●	●	●	●	●	●	●	●	●	●
C Using New Words in Context	●	●	●	●	●	●	●	●	●	●	●	●
Focus on Skills												
Giving Reasons			D		D							E
Story Structure				D				D		D		
Character Feelings		D				D	D					
Antonyms	E								E			D
Punctuation							E	E		E		
Suffixes		E		E		E						
Compound Words	D				E						E	
Blends			E						D		D	

Olive	Power Builder Number											
	1	2	3	4	5	6	7	8	9	10	11	12
Ⓐ Build Comprehension	**Item Numbers**											
Identifying the Main Idea	1	1	1	1	1	1	1	1	1	1	1	1
Drawing Conclusions	4	2, 3, 4	3	2, 3	5	2, 3		2, 3	2, 5		4	2
Making Inferences			4					5	4	2, 5	2, 3, 5	5
Understanding Cause and Effect	5		2, 5		3	5	2, 5	4	3			
Comparing and Contrasting	2, 3	5			4	4						
Predicting Outcomes				4			4					
Identifying Literary Elements				5	2		3			3, 4		3, 4
Learn about Words												
Ⓑ Word Meaning in Context	●	●	●	●	●	●	●	●	●	●	●	●
Ⓒ Using New Words in Context	●	●	●	●	●	●	●	●	●	●	●	●
Focus on Skills												
Topic Details	E								D			E
Sequence		D			D		D					
Character Feelings			D							E		
Classification				D		E					D	
Past Tense		E						D	E		E	
Pronoun Antecedents	D			E						D		
Contractions			E			D		E				
Possessives					E		E					D

Aqua	Power Builder Number											
	1	2	3	4	5	6	7	8	9	10	11	12
A Build Comprehension	Item Numbers											
Identifying the Main Idea	1	1	1	1	1	1	1	1	1	1	1	1
Drawing Conclusions	5	4		2, 3, 4	5		3, 4		2	3, 4		4
Making Inferences			3					5	5			2
Understanding Cause and Effect	2, 3	5				4			3, 4		4	3, 5
Comparing and Contrasting		2								2	2, 3	
Predicting Outcomes	4	3	5	5								
Identifying Literary Elements			2, 4		2, 3, 4		2, 5	2			5	
Recognizing Problems and Solutions						2, 3, 5		3, 4		5		
Learn about Words												
B Word Meaning in Context	●	●	●	●	●	●	●	●	●	●	●	●
C Word Relationships	●	●	●	●	●	●	●	●	●	●	●	●
Focus on Skills												
Story Map			D		D					D		
Fact or Opinion	D					D				E		
Classification		D		D					D		D	
Analogies							D					D
Inflectional Endings			E		E			E				
Irregular Plurals	E						E	D				
Suffixes		E							E			E
Alphabetical Order				E		E					E	

Blue	Power Builder Number											
	1	2	3	4	5	6	7	8	9	10	11	12
A Build Comprehension	Item Numbers											
Identifying the Main Idea	1	1	1	1	1	1	1	1	1	1	1	1
Drawing Conclusions		3, 4, 5	4	5	2, 3	3, 5	3		2, 5			2
Making Inferences			5				5	3, 5	4	4	2	
Understanding Cause and Effect	4		3	4		4	2	2				
Comparing and Contrasting	3		2	2, 3			4		3	2, 3, 5	3, 4	
Predicting Outcomes								4			5	3
Identifying Literary Elements					4, 5							4, 5
Recognizing Problems and Solutions	2, 5	2				2						
Learn about Words												
B Word Meaning in Context	●	●	●	●	●	●	●	●	●	●	●	●
C Word Relationships	●	●	●	●	●	●	●	●	●	●	●	●
Focus on Skills												
Story Map					E			E				D
Classification	D					D				D		
Sequence		D										
Fact or Opinion				E					E			
Antonyms										E		
Idioms			D								D	
Inflectional Endings	E					E						E
Contractions			E				E					
Prefixes and Suffixes					D		D	D			E	
Pronoun Antecedents		E		D					D			

Purple	Power Builder Number											
	1	2	3	4	5	6	7	8	9	10	11	12
A Build Comprehension	**Item Numbers**											
Identifying the Main Idea	1	1	1	1	1	1	1	1	1	1	1	1
Drawing Conclusions		3	4	2, 3		4, 5	2, 5	3			3	2, 3, 4
Making Inferences			2	5		2		5	3	2, 4		
Understanding Cause and Effect	2	4	3		3		4			3		5
Comparing and Contrasting	3, 4				4	3	3		2, 4	5	2, 4, 5	
Predicting Outcomes	5	5	5	4	5				5			
Identifying Literary Elements		2			2			2, 4				
Learn about Words												
B Word Meaning in Context	●	●	●	●	●	●	●	●	●	●	●	●
C Word Relationships	●	●	●	●	●	●	●	●	●	●	●	●
Focus on Skills												
Topic Details						F		E	F			
Sequence					D							D
Fact or Opinion	D	E				E	D	D				
Character Feelings		F	D									
Classification				D					E	F	E	
Comparisons	F			F								F
Past Tense			F		F							
Antonyms and Synonyms	E	D					F		D	E	F	
Prefixes and Suffixes						D		F		D	D	
Possessive Pronouns			E									E
Contractions				E	E		E					

Violet	Power Builder Number											
	1	2	3	4	5	6	7	8	9	10	11	12
A Build Comprehension	Item Numbers											
Identifying the Main Idea	1	1	1	1	1	1	1	1	1	1	1	1
Drawing Conclusions		2, 5	2, 4		2, 4	3		5		3, 5	5	
Making Inferences	4, 5		5		3		2, 4	2				
Understanding Cause and Effect	3					4		3	2, 3		2, 3	4, 5
Comparing and Contrasting		4	3	2	5	2, 5		4			4	2, 3
Predicting Outcomes		3		4			5		5			
Identifying Literary Elements	2			3			3		4	2, 4		
Recognizing Problems and Solutions				5								
Learn about Words												
B Word Meaning in Context	●	●	●	●	●	●	●	●	●	●	●	●
C Word Relationships	●	●	●	●	●	●	●	●	●	●	●	●
Focus on Skills												
Story Map							E		E			
Sequence			D					D		D		
Fact or Opinion			E		F						D	
Character Feelings		D		D		D						
Classification						F				F		F
Comparisons	D										E	
Idioms									D			
Irregular Past Tense				F		E		F				
Antonyms					D		F	E				D
Suffixes	E						D					E
Possessive Pronouns		E		E					F			
Contractions	F		F								F	
Irregular Plurals		F			E					E		

Student Resources

The following section contains resources for your students. You will copy and distribute these materials as needed. These resources include:

- Home Connection Letter–As you begin ***SRA Reading Laboratory*** with your students, copy the home connection letter and distribute it to students to take home and share with their parents or guardians.
- Starter Stories–These stories will be used to determine the color level at which each student should enter the ***Power Builder*** component.
- Record Page–Students write their answers to the ***Power Builder*** questions on these pages.
- Progress Charts–These allow students and you to track their progress as they work through the ***Power Builders***.

Ordering SRA Reading Laboratory® Student Record Books

In place of using the materials in the Student Resources section, keep students organized with their own individual books. Students can use their books to record answers to questions, correct their work, and record their scores and progress, promoting student accountability and ownership. To order printed copies of the Student Record Book, please visit: **https://www.mheducation.com/prek-12/explore/create-easy-order.** You can quickly find the appropriate level Student Record Book by searching for ISBN 9781309122013.

Home Connection Letter

This school year your child will be using the ***SRA Reading Laboratory*** program. This multileveled system of individualized instruction will provide your child with reading practice.

SRA Reading Laboratory offers high-interest fiction and nonfiction reading passages that cover a wide range of topics. The reading passages are divided into levels. Each level is represented by a different color, and each color is more difficult to read than the previous color.

Your child will move through the levels at his or her own pace, while working toward the following goals:

- To develop comprehension, vocabulary, word analysis, and study skills
- To reinforce specific skills to help your child become a proficient reader
- To interest your child in reading and to enlarge his or her specific knowledge, using a wide array of quality fiction and nonfiction selections
- To develop as an independent reader with strong comprehension skills, endurance, and confidence
- To develop the sense of personal responsibility by taking charge of his or her own learning

Millions of students have been using and enjoying ***SRA Reading Laboratory*** over the years. I'm sure your child will enjoy it too.

The Old Tree

There is an old tree on the hill. It is strong and tall. It is like a city. The tree is home for many animals.

Squirrels live up high in it. Raccoons and bees live in its holes. Rabbits live under it. The animals store food in it. They raise their babies there. Its leaves are their roof. The trunk is their floor.

The tree helps them. It keeps the rain and wind out. It keeps them safe. It is a fine place to live!

Build Comprehension

A Read each question. Write *a* or *b*.

1. What is this story about?
   a. How a tree is a home to animals
   b. Why old trees grow so tall
2. How is an old tree like a city?
   a. It helps humans who are close by.
   b. It has many spaces for animal homes.
3. What are the holes in the tree good for?
   a. Keeping animals and food from getting wet
   b. Helping the tree stay green and strong
4. How are rabbits not like raccoons?
   a. Rabbits don't go up into trees.
   b. Rabbits want their babies to be safe.
5. Why do animals live in the old tree?
   a. Because there are no other homes for them
   b. Because they have safe homes there

Learn about Words

B s + ad = sad

Say the word *sad*. Listen to the sound of *ad*. Then look at the letters in the box. Add each letter to *ad* to make a word. Write the word.

1. m	
2. h	+ ad
3. gl	

C **Read the words you wrote. Which one best fits in each sentence? Write the word.**

4. The hill ___ an old tree on it.
5. The animals are ___ it keeps the rain out.
6. I will be ___ if a bee stings me.

Focus on Skills

D **Here are things people say about birds. If the sentence tells why birds live in trees, write *Yes*. If it does not tell why birds live in trees, write *No*.**

1. Trees keep birds safe.
2. Trees need rain and sun.
3. Trees have places for nests.
4. Trees keep wind and rain out.

Dragon Mountain

A fire burned on Dragon Mountain. This fire scared the dragons who lived there. They tried to put it out, but the fire just spread.

Walter began to cry. His tears made a pool. Looking at the pool, Walter had an idea!

"Everyone cry!" he shouted.

"Why?" asked the dragons.

"You'll see," said Walter.

The dragons cried. Their big tears fell into the pool. The pool became a lake. The lake got bigger. It soon reached the fire. The fire went out.

The dragons hugged Walter.

Build Comprehension

A **Read each question. Write *a* or *b*.**

1. What is another good name for this story?
   a. Walter's Funny Idea
   b. A Lake of Tears
2. Why does Walter cry at first?
   a. Because he is afraid of the fire
   b. Because the other dragons tell him to
3. What is Walter's idea?
   a. To have the dragons go to a higher mountain
   b. To have the dragons put out the fire with tears
4. Why is Walter's idea a good one?
   a. Because mountains have lakes
   b. Because water puts out fire
5. Why do the dragons hug Walter?
   a. Because his idea works
   b. Because he is crying

Learn about Words

B **g + ame = game**

Say the word *game.* Listen to the sound of *ame.* Then look at the letters in the box. Add each letter to *ame* to make a word. Write the word.

1. n	
2. c	**+ ame**
3. s	

C **Read the words you wrote. Which one best fits in each sentence? Write the word.**

4. The fire ________ closer.
5. The dragon's ________ was Walter.
6. All the dragons cried at the ________ time.

Focus on Skills

D **Read each sentence. Which word in the box means almost the same thing as the underlined word? Write the word.**

dropped	pond	larger	started

1. A fire <u>began</u> to burn on Dragon Mountain.
2. The dragons' tears <u>fell</u> into the pool.
3. The pool grew <u>bigger</u>.
4. The tears soon made a <u>lake</u>.

Our Pet, Noise

We went for a ride in the country. We ate our lunch in the woods and had so much fun! We packed the car for the long return to home. As we drove down a very bumpy road, we heard a funny noise. Was something loose or stuck to the car? Grandma stopped the car to check. She got out and looked around and under the car. Nothing looked out of place. What was the noise?

We drove home. When we got there, we opened the trunk of the car. A small rabbit was making the funny noise! We call her Noise, and now she's our pet.

Build Comprehension

A **Read each question. Write *a* or *b*.**

1. What is the story about?
   a. Going for a ride
   b. Finding a surprise
2. When does the rabbit most likely get into the car?
   a. When they pack the car to go home
   b. When Grandma looks under the car
3. Why does the car make a funny noise?
   a. Because the car has a big rock in it
   b. Because the car has an animal in it
4. Why do they open the trunk of the car?
   a. To get their things out of the car
   b. To find the rabbit
5. Why does the family name the rabbit Noise?
   a. Because the rabbit makes the noise in the car
   b. Because rabbits are very noisy animals

Learn about Words

B s + et = set

Say the word *set.* Listen to the sound of *et.* Then look at the letters in the box. Add each letter to *et* to make a word. Write the word.

1. g	
2. y	
3. m	**+ et**
4. l	
5. p	

C Read the words you wrote. Which one best fits in each sentence? Write the word.

6. Have you ________ my grandma?
7. Noise is the name of our ________.
8. Noise does not have any babies ________.
9. Let's ________ some food for Noise.
10. Please ________ me hold Noise.

Focus on Skills

D Word pictures help you see things more clearly. They tell you more about a story. Choose the sentence that gives a better picture. Write *a* or *b*.

1. **a.** We had fun playing tag and ball in the park.
   b. We had fun playing games.
2. **a.** The road was not very good.
   b. The road was old and bumpy.
3. **a.** Grandma looked around.
   b. Grandma looked under the car.
4. **a.** The rabbit moved around a lot.
   b. The rabbit hopped and jumped.

The Duck in the Park

A duck was happily playing a guitar. He really liked music.

A man heard the music. When he saw the duck playing he was very surprised. "Duck!" he called. "What do you think you're doing?"

"I'm playing a guitar," smiled the duck as he played a pretty French song.

"But you are a duck!" said the man, frowning.

"Yes, I am," nodded the duck. He played a happy English song.

"A duck playing a guitar?" the man said.

The duck played a slow German song.

The man was very upset.

The duck played a fast Spanish song.

"This is impossible!" the man shouted. "Ducks cannot play guitars!"

"I didn't know that," the duck said sadly. He put the guitar down. He never played it again.

But I think he should have, don't you?

Build Comprehension

A Read each question. Write *a* or *b*.

1. What does the duck do in this story?
   a. He gives up something he shouldn't have.
   b. He gives his guitar to a man.
2. What is a guitar?
   a. Something to make music with
   b. A pretty French song
3. Why is the man surprised?
   a. Because he has never seen a duck in the park before
   b. Because he doesn't think an animal can make music
4. Why does the duck stop playing?
   a. Because he lets the man tell him what to do
   b. Because he does not know how to play anymore
5. What should the duck do to be happy?
   a. Tell the man that he is right
   b. Start playing the guitar again

Learn about Words

B f + an = fan

Say the word *fan*. Listen to the sound of *an*. Then look at the letters in the box. Add each letter to *an* to make a word. Write the word.

1. c	
2. m	
3. r	+ an
4. t	
5. pl	

C **Read the words you wrote. Which one best fits in each sentence? Write the word.**

6. The man wore a black and ________ shirt.
7. The duck's ________ was to be a guitar player.
8. The duck ________ play many kinds of music.
9. People ________ by the duck as he played.
10. The ________ was surprised to see the duck.

Focus on Skills

D ***Day*** **and** ***say*** **end the same way. They rhyme. Read each pair of sentences. Which word in ( ) rhymes with the underlined word? Write the word.**

1. The duck played a song.
   The man thought that was (right, wrong).
2. The man was sure ducks couldn't play.
   He got a surprise that (day, time).
3. The man was so upset he began to hop.
   He told the duck to (stop, leave).
4. The man began to frown.
   The duck put the guitar (down, away).

Once More for Baby!

"Mom and dad are outside working in the yard. Will you watch baby Jack while I wash the windows?" Sam asked.

"All right," said his sister. She put the baby on a blanket on the floor and sat down beside him to read.

Jack was unhappy, so he cried and fussed.

Sam's sister tickled the baby. She even made faces, but nothing helped.

"Help me cheer him up," she said. "Nothing I do makes him happy."

"Sorry—that's your job," said Sam. "I've got to wash the windows."

Sam got a stepladder and a bucket of water. He climbed to the top of a window and started to wash it.

Creak! The ladder began to lean.

Crash! The ladder fell!

Bump! Down came Sam!

Thump! The bucket came down beside him!

Squish! A wet rag landed on his face!

Ouch! Sam hurt all over!

His sister cheered. "Oh, Sam! Do it again! You made Jack laugh!"

Build Comprehension

A Choose the best ending for each sentence. Write *a* or *b*.

1. This story is supposed to
   a. teach you something.
   b. make you laugh.
2. Sam's sister makes faces because
   a. she really wants to wash the windows.
   b. she wants to cheer the baby up.
3. Sam climbs the ladder because
   a. he can't reach the top of the windows.
   b. he can see the baby better from there.
4. Jack most likely laughs because
   a. Sam looks silly.
   b. Sam tells a joke.
5. The funny part of this story is that
   a. Sam's sister tickles Jack.
   b. Sam isn't trying to make Jack laugh.

Learn about Words

B *Waterfall* is a word that is made from two smaller words, *water* and *fall. Waterfall* is a compound word.

Put the smaller words together to make a compound word. Write the compound word.

1. step + ladder = _______
2. him + self = _______
3. baby + sit = _______
4. bath + room = _______
5. every + one = _______

C Read the new words you wrote. Which one best fits in each sentence? Write the word.

6. _______ but Sam thought his fall was funny.
7. Sam did not want to _______ the baby.
8. Sam prepared _______ for cleaning the windows.
9. Sam cleaned up in the _______ after his fall.
10. Dad used the _______ to change a burned-out light.

Focus on Skills

D **Read each story. Write *a* or *b* to answer question.**

The baby was hungry. Mother warmed a bottle of milk. Mother sat in a chair with the baby.

1. What will Mother probably do next?
   a. Read the baby a story
   b. Give the bottle to the baby
2. What will the baby probably do next?
   a. Play with toys
   b. Drink the milk
3. How do you know what Mother and baby will do?
   a. Mother warms a bottle. The baby is hungry.
   b. Mother sits in a chair. The baby likes toys.

Sam got a bucket of soapy water. Then he got a rag. He took them into the kitchen.

4. What will Sam probably do next?
   a. Clean the kitchen
   b. Make his lunch
5. How do you know what Sam will do?
   a. He is hungry.
   b. He gets soapy water and a rag.

Mud, Lovely Mud

1 Children in Hawaii can't go sledding, and they can't play in the snow. Why? There isn't any snow there because the weather is warm all year. But they have another sport, and it's just as good. Maybe it's better. It's mud sliding.

2 Mud sliding is a lot like sledding, but there's no snowy hill, and there's no sled. There is a muddy slope and a big bunch of leaves the children sit on.

3 Ti plants grow in the forest. These plants have long, broad leaves on a thick stem. When it rains in the forest, the rainwater makes mud. Each slider cuts off a branch of leaves and climbs to the top of a muddy slope.

4 The sliders put a ti branch between their legs, using it like a broomstick horse. They sit on the leaves and hold on to the stem.

5 Then they let themselves go. The riders of the leafy sleds take off as they zip down the slope, going faster and faster.

6 The ride is over too soon! When the sliders reach the bottom, they seem to be all mud and smiles.

7 But the fun isn't over. Everyone heads for the nearest stream. The sliders splash and play in the water, all while getting clean at the same time!

Build Comprehension

A Choose the best ending for each sentence. Write *a* or *b*.

1. This story is about
   a. one way people have fun in Hawaii.
   b. the only way people get clean in Hawaii.
2. Before people can go mud sliding,
   a. it has to get hot.
   b. it has to rain.
3. A mud slider must first
   a. splash in a close-by stream.
   b. cut a leaf from a ti plant.
4. A ti leaf is like a sled because
   a. both need snow to slide on.
   b. both slide down hills well.
5. Once the rides are over, everyone goes to a stream
   a. to wash the mud off and have more fun.
   b. to get a drink of water and cut more leaves.

Learn about Words

B Often you can find out the meaning of a word by seeing how it is used in a story. The other words in the story give you clues.

Find the word in the story that best fits each meaning. (A paragraph number tells you where to look.) Write the word.

1. using an object to slide down a snowy hill (1)
2. hill (2)
3. stack (2)
4. wide (3)
5. move quickly (5)

C Read each sentence. Choose the word from Part B that best completes each sentence.

6. My dog likes to _______ around the yard.
7. I can't believe how _______ this tree trunk is.
8. _______ is my favorite activity on a snowy day.
9. Dad put a _______ of cardboard boxes in the recycling bin.
10. I will need better shoes to climb that _______.

Focus on Skills

D **Look at the story map below. Complete the story map by writing the letter that tells in what order each event happened.**

a. ______

↓

b. ______

↓

c. ______

↓

d. ______

↓

e. ______

1. Sliders clean off in a stream. ________
2. Sliders sit on a branch of ti leaves. ________
3. Sliders go to the top of a muddy slope. ________
4. Rain falls in Hawaii. ________
5. Sliders go down the muddy slope. ________

E **Why do they slide on mud? There is no snow in Hawaii. How fast they go!**

A sentence that asks a question ends with a question mark (?). A sentence that tells something ends with a period (.). A sentence that tells something with strong feeling ends with an exclamation point (!).

Read each sentence. If it should end with a question mark, write *question.* If it should end with a *period,* write period. If it should end with an exclamation point, write *exclamation.*

6. Mud sliding is a lot like snow sledding
7. What do people use for sleds
8. They use a ti leaf
9. Look out for that tree
10. Where can I go mud sliding

Record Page

Name ______________________ Date __________

Power Builder Color ______________ Power Builder Number ________

Ⓐ Build Comprehension

1. ________ 2. ________ 3. ________ 4. ________ 5. ________

Number Correct ☐

Ⓑ Ⓒ Learn about Words

1. ______________________ 6. ______________________

2. ______________________ 7. ______________________

3. ______________________ 8. ______________________

4. ______________________ 9. ______________________

5. ______________________ 10. ______________________

Number Correct ☐

Ⓓ Ⓔ Ⓕ Focus on Skills

1. ____________ 6. ____________ 11. ____________

2. ____________ 7. ____________ 12. ____________

3. ____________ 8. ____________ 13. ____________

4. ____________ 9. ____________ 14. ____________

5. ____________ 10. ____________ 15. ____________

Number Correct ☐

My Reading Progress Chart: Red Level

Fill in the box for each correct answer on your Power Builder.

Power Builder Number	Date	(A) Build Comprehension	(B) (C) Learn about Words	(D) Focus on Skills
		1 2 3 4 5	1 2 3 4 5 6	1 2 3 4
		1 2 3 4 5	1 2 3 4 5 6	1 2 3 4
		1 2 3 4 5	1 2 3 4 5 6	1 2 3 4
		1 2 3 4 5	1 2 3 4 5 6	1 2 3 4
		1 2 3 4 5	1 2 3 4 5 6	1 2 3 4
		1 2 3 4 5	1 2 3 4 5 6	1 2 3 4
		1 2 3 4 5	1 2 3 4 5 6	1 2 3 4
		1 2 3 4 5	1 2 3 4 5 6	1 2 3 4
		1 2 3 4 5	1 2 3 4 5 6	1 2 3 4
		1 2 3 4 5	1 2 3 4 5 6	1 2 3 4
		1 2 3 4 5	1 2 3 4 5 6	1 2 3 4
		1 2 3 4 5	1 2 3 4 5 6	1 2 3 4

My Reading Progress Chart: Orange Level

Fill in the box for each correct answer on your Power Builder.

Power Builder Number	Date	A Build Comprehension	B C Learn about Words	D Focus on Skills
		1 2 3 4 5	1 2 3 4 5 6 7 8 9 10	1 2 3 4
		1 2 3 4 5	1 2 3 4 5 6 7 8 9 10	1 2 3 4
		1 2 3 4 5	1 2 3 4 5 6 7 8 9 10	1 2 3 4
		1 2 3 4 5	1 2 3 4 5 6 7 8 9 10	1 2 3 4
		1 2 3 4 5	1 2 3 4 5 6 7 8 9 10	1 2 3 4
		1 2 3 4 5	1 2 3 4 5 6 7 8 9 10	1 2 3 4
		1 2 3 4 5	1 2 3 4 5 6 7 8 9 10	1 2 3 4
		1 2 3 4 5	1 2 3 4 5 6 7 8 9 10	1 2 3 4
		1 2 3 4 5	1 2 3 4 5 6 7 8 9 10	1 2 3 4
		1 2 3 4 5	1 2 3 4 5 6 7 8 9 10	1 2 3 4
		1 2 3 4 5	1 2 3 4 5 6 7 8 9 10	1 2 3 4
		1 2 3 4 5	1 2 3 4 5 6 7 8 9 10	1 2 3 4

My Reading Progress Chart: Gold Level

Fill in the box for each correct answer on your Power Builder.

Power Builder Number	Date	A Build Comprehension					B C Learn about Words										D Focus on Skills			
		1	2	3	4	5	1	2	3	4	5	6	7	8	9	10	1	2	3	4
		1	2	3	4	5	1	2	3	4	5	6	7	8	9	10	1	2	3	4
		1	2	3	4	5	1	2	3	4	5	6	7	8	9	10	1	2	3	4
		1	2	3	4	5	1	2	3	4	5	6	7	8	9	10	1	2	3	4
		1	2	3	4	5	1	2	3	4	5	6	7	8	9	10	1	2	3	4
		1	2	3	4	5	1	2	3	4	5	6	7	8	9	10	1	2	3	4
		1	2	3	4	5	1	2	3	4	5	6	7	8	9	10	1	2	3	4
		1	2	3	4	5	1	2	3	4	5	6	7	8	9	10	1	2	3	4
		1	2	3	4	5	1	2	3	4	5	6	7	8	9	10	1	2	3	4
		1	2	3	4	5	1	2	3	4	5	6	7	8	9	10	1	2	3	4
		1	2	3	4	5	1	2	3	4	5	6	7	8	9	10	1	2	3	4
		1	2	3	4	5	1	2	3	4	5	6	7	8	9	10	1	2	3	4

My Reading Progress Chart: **Brown Level**

Fill in the box for each correct answer on your Power Builder.

Power Builder Number	Date	Ⓐ Build Comprehension					Ⓑ Ⓒ Learn about Words										Ⓓ Focus on Skills				
		1	2	3	4	5	1	2	3	4	5	6	7	8	9	10	1	2	3	4	5
		1	2	3	4	5	1	2	3	4	5	6	7	8	9	10	1	2	3	4	5
		1	2	3	4	5	1	2	3	4	5	6	7	8	9	10	1	2	3	4	5
		1	2	3	4	5	1	2	3	4	5	6	7	8	9	10	1	2	3	4	5
		1	2	3	4	5	1	2	3	4	5	6	7	8	9	10	1	2	3	4	5
		1	2	3	4	5	1	2	3	4	5	6	7	8	9	10	1	2	3	4	5
		1	2	3	4	5	1	2	3	4	5	6	7	8	9	10	1	2	3	4	5
		1	2	3	4	5	1	2	3	4	5	6	7	8	9	10	1	2	3	4	5
		1	2	3	4	5	1	2	3	4	5	6	7	8	9	10	1	2	3	4	5
		1	2	3	4	5	1	2	3	4	5	6	7	8	9	10	1	2	3	4	5
		1	2	3	4	5	1	2	3	4	5	6	7	8	9	10	1	2	3	4	5
		1	2	3	4	5	1	2	3	4	5	6	7	8	9	10	1	2	3	4	5

My Reading Progress Chart: Tan Level

Fill in the box for each correct answer on your Power Builder.

Power Builder Number	Date	Ⓐ Build Comprehension	Ⓑ Ⓒ Learn about Words	Ⓓ Focus on Skills
		1 2 3 4 5	1 2 3 4 5 6 7 8 9 10	1 2 3 4 5
		1 2 3 4 5	1 2 3 4 5 6 7 8 9 10	1 2 3 4 5
		1 2 3 4 5	1 2 3 4 5 6 7 8 9 10	1 2 3 4 5
		1 2 3 4 5	1 2 3 4 5 6 7 8 9 10	1 2 3 4 5
		1 2 3 4 5	1 2 3 4 5 6 7 8 9 10	1 2 3 4 5
		1 2 3 4 5	1 2 3 4 5 6 7 8 9 10	1 2 3 4 5
		1 2 3 4 5	1 2 3 4 5 6 7 8 9 10	1 2 3 4 5
		1 2 3 4 5	1 2 3 4 5 6 7 8 9 10	1 2 3 4 5
		1 2 3 4 5	1 2 3 4 5 6 7 8 9 10	1 2 3 4 5
		1 2 3 4 5	1 2 3 4 5 6 7 8 9 10	1 2 3 4 5
		1 2 3 4 5	1 2 3 4 5 6 7 8 9 10	1 2 3 4 5
		1 2 3 4 5	1 2 3 4 5 6 7 8 9 10	1 2 3 4 5

My Reading Progress Chart: Lime Level

Fill in the box for each correct answer on your Power Builder.

Power Builder Number	Date	Ⓐ Build Comprehension	Ⓑ Ⓒ Learn about Words	Ⓓ Ⓔ Focus on Skills
		1 2 3 4 5	1 2 3 4 5 6 7 8 9 10	1 2 3 4 5 6 7 8 9 10
		1 2 3 4 5	1 2 3 4 5 6 7 8 9 10	1 2 3 4 5 6 7 8 9 10
		1 2 3 4 5	1 2 3 4 5 6 7 8 9 10	1 2 3 4 5 6 7 8 9 10
		1 2 3 4 5	1 2 3 4 5 6 7 8 9 10	1 2 3 4 5 6 7 8 9 10
		1 2 3 4 5	1 2 3 4 5 6 7 8 9 10	1 2 3 4 5 6 7 8 9 10
		1 2 3 4 5	1 2 3 4 5 6 7 8 9 10	1 2 3 4 5 6 7 8 9 10
		1 2 3 4 5	1 2 3 4 5 6 7 8 9 10	1 2 3 4 5 6 7 8 9 10
		1 2 3 4 5	1 2 3 4 5 6 7 8 9 10	1 2 3 4 5 6 7 8 9 10
		1 2 3 4 5	1 2 3 4 5 6 7 8 9 10	1 2 3 4 5 6 7 8 9 10
		1 2 3 4 5	1 2 3 4 5 6 7 8 9 10	1 2 3 4 5 6 7 8 9 10
		1 2 3 4 5	1 2 3 4 5 6 7 8 9 10	1 2 3 4 5 6 7 8 9 10
		1 2 3 4 5	1 2 3 4 5 6 7 8 9 10	1 2 3 4 5 6 7 8 9 10

My Reading Progress Chart: Green Level

Fill in the box for each correct answer on your Power Builder.

Power Builder Number	Date	Ⓐ Build Comprehension	ⒷⒸ Learn about Words	ⒹⒺ Focus on Skills
		1 2 3 4 5	1 2 3 4 5 6 7 8 9 10	1 2 3 4 5 6 7 8 9 10
		1 2 3 4 5	1 2 3 4 5 6 7 8 9 10	1 2 3 4 5 6 7 8 9 10
		1 2 3 4 5	1 2 3 4 5 6 7 8 9 10	1 2 3 4 5 6 7 8 9 10
		1 2 3 4 5	1 2 3 4 5 6 7 8 9 10	1 2 3 4 5 6 7 8 9 10
		1 2 3 4 5	1 2 3 4 5 6 7 8 9 10	1 2 3 4 5 6 7 8 9 10
		1 2 3 4 5	1 2 3 4 5 6 7 8 9 10	1 2 3 4 5 6 7 8 9 10
		1 2 3 4 5	1 2 3 4 5 6 7 8 9 10	1 2 3 4 5 6 7 8 9 10
		1 2 3 4 5	1 2 3 4 5 6 7 8 9 10	1 2 3 4 5 6 7 8 9 10
		1 2 3 4 5	1 2 3 4 5 6 7 8 9 10	1 2 3 4 5 6 7 8 9 10
		1 2 3 4 5	1 2 3 4 5 6 7 8 9 10	1 2 3 4 5 6 7 8 9 10
		1 2 3 4 5	1 2 3 4 5 6 7 8 9 10	1 2 3 4 5 6 7 8 9 10
		1 2 3 4 5	1 2 3 4 5 6 7 8 9 10	1 2 3 4 5 6 7 8 9 10

My Reading Progress Chart: Olive Level

Fill in the box for each correct answer on your Power Builder.

Power Builder Number	Date	Ⓐ Build Comprehension	Ⓑ Ⓒ Learn about Words	Ⓓ Ⓔ Focus on Skills
		1 2 3 4 5	1 2 3 4 5 6 7 8 9 10	1 2 3 4 5 6 7 8 9 10
		1 2 3 4 5	1 2 3 4 5 6 7 8 9 10	1 2 3 4 5 6 7 8 9 10
		1 2 3 4 5	1 2 3 4 5 6 7 8 9 10	1 2 3 4 5 6 7 8 9 10
		1 2 3 4 5	1 2 3 4 5 6 7 8 9 10	1 2 3 4 5 6 7 8 9 10
		1 2 3 4 5	1 2 3 4 5 6 7 8 9 10	1 2 3 4 5 6 7 8 9 10
		1 2 3 4 5	1 2 3 4 5 6 7 8 9 10	1 2 3 4 5 6 7 8 9 10
		1 2 3 4 5	1 2 3 4 5 6 7 8 9 10	1 2 3 4 5 6 7 8 9 10
		1 2 3 4 5	1 2 3 4 5 6 7 8 9 10	1 2 3 4 5 6 7 8 9 10
		1 2 3 4 5	1 2 3 4 5 6 7 8 9 10	1 2 3 4 5 6 7 8 9 10
		1 2 3 4 5	1 2 3 4 5 6 7 8 9 10	1 2 3 4 5 6 7 8 9 10
		1 2 3 4 5	1 2 3 4 5 6 7 8 9 10	1 2 3 4 5 6 7 8 9 10
		1 2 3 4 5	1 2 3 4 5 6 7 8 9 10	1 2 3 4 5 6 7 8 9 10

My Reading Progress Chart: Aqua Level

Fill in the box for each correct answer on your Power Builder.

Power Builder Number	Date	A Build Comprehension	B C Learn about Words	D E Focus on Skills
		1 2 3 4 5	1 2 3 4 5 6 7 8 9 10	1 2 3 4 5 6 7 8 9 10
		1 2 3 4 5	1 2 3 4 5 6 7 8 9 10	1 2 3 4 5 6 7 8 9 10
		1 2 3 4 5	1 2 3 4 5 6 7 8 9 10	1 2 3 4 5 6 7 8 9 10
		1 2 3 4 5	1 2 3 4 5 6 7 8 9 10	1 2 3 4 5 6 7 8 9 10
		1 2 3 4 5	1 2 3 4 5 6 7 8 9 10	1 2 3 4 5 6 7 8 9 10
		1 2 3 4 5	1 2 3 4 5 6 7 8 9 10	1 2 3 4 5 6 7 8 9 10
		1 2 3 4 5	1 2 3 4 5 6 7 8 9 10	1 2 3 4 5 6 7 8 9 10
		1 2 3 4 5	1 2 3 4 5 6 7 8 9 10	1 2 3 4 5 6 7 8 9 10
		1 2 3 4 5	1 2 3 4 5 6 7 8 9 10	1 2 3 4 5 6 7 8 9 10
		1 2 3 4 5	1 2 3 4 5 6 7 8 9 10	1 2 3 4 5 6 7 8 9 10
		1 2 3 4 5	1 2 3 4 5 6 7 8 9 10	1 2 3 4 5 6 7 8 9 10
		1 2 3 4 5	1 2 3 4 5 6 7 8 9 10	1 2 3 4 5 6 7 8 9 10

My Reading Progress Chart: Blue Level

Fill in the box for each correct answer on your Power Builder.

Power Builder Number	Date	A Build Comprehension	B C Learn about Words	D E Focus on Skills
		1 2 3 4 5	1 2 3 4 5 6 7 8 9 10	1 2 3 4 5 6 7 8 9 10
		1 2 3 4 5	1 2 3 4 5 6 7 8 9 10	1 2 3 4 5 6 7 8 9 10
		1 2 3 4 5	1 2 3 4 5 6 7 8 9 10	1 2 3 4 5 6 7 8 9 10
		1 2 3 4 5	1 2 3 4 5 6 7 8 9 10	1 2 3 4 5 6 7 8 9 10
		1 2 3 4 5	1 2 3 4 5 6 7 8 9 10	1 2 3 4 5 6 7 8 9 10
		1 2 3 4 5	1 2 3 4 5 6 7 8 9 10	1 2 3 4 5 6 7 8 9 10
		1 2 3 4 5	1 2 3 4 5 6 7 8 9 10	1 2 3 4 5 6 7 8 9 10
		1 2 3 4 5	1 2 3 4 5 6 7 8 9 10	1 2 3 4 5 6 7 8 9 10
		1 2 3 4 5	1 2 3 4 5 6 7 8 9 10	1 2 3 4 5 6 7 8 9 10
		1 2 3 4 5	1 2 3 4 5 6 7 8 9 10	1 2 3 4 5 6 7 8 9 10
		1 2 3 4 5	1 2 3 4 5 6 7 8 9 10	1 2 3 4 5 6 7 8 9 10
		1 2 3 4 5	1 2 3 4 5 6 7 8 9 10	1 2 3 4 5 6 7 8 9 10

My Reading Progress Chart: **Purple Level**

Fill in the box for each correct answer on your Power Builder.

Power Builder Number	Date	Ⓐ Build Comprehension	Ⓑ Ⓒ Learn about Words	Ⓓ Ⓔ Ⓕ Focus on Skills
		1 2 3 4 5	1 2 3 4 5 6 7 8 9 10	1 2 3 4 5 6 7 8 9 10 11 12 13 14 15
		1 2 3 4 5	1 2 3 4 5 6 7 8 9 10	1 2 3 4 5 6 7 8 9 10 11 12 13 14 15
		1 2 3 4 5	1 2 3 4 5 6 7 8 9 10	1 2 3 4 5 6 7 8 9 10 11 12 13 14 15
		1 2 3 4 5	1 2 3 4 5 6 7 8 9 10	1 2 3 4 5 6 7 8 9 10 11 12 13 14 15
		1 2 3 4 5	1 2 3 4 5 6 7 8 9 10	1 2 3 4 5 6 7 8 9 10 11 12 13 14 15
		1 2 3 4 5	1 2 3 4 5 6 7 8 9 10	1 2 3 4 5 6 7 8 9 10 11 12 13 14 15
		1 2 3 4 5	1 2 3 4 5 6 7 8 9 10	1 2 3 4 5 6 7 8 9 10 11 12 13 14 15
		1 2 3 4 5	1 2 3 4 5 6 7 8 9 10	1 2 3 4 5 6 7 8 9 10 11 12 13 14 15
		1 2 3 4 5	1 2 3 4 5 6 7 8 9 10	1 2 3 4 5 6 7 8 9 10 11 12 13 14 15
		1 2 3 4 5	1 2 3 4 5 6 7 8 9 10	1 2 3 4 5 6 7 8 9 10 11 12 13 14 15
		1 2 3 4 5	1 2 3 4 5 6 7 8 9 10	1 2 3 4 5 6 7 8 9 10 11 12 13 14 15
		1 2 3 4 5	1 2 3 4 5 6 7 8 9 10	1 2 3 4 5 6 7 8 9 10 11 12 13 14 15

My Reading Progress Chart: Violet Level

Fill in the box for each correct answer on your Power Builder.

Power Builder Number	Date	A Build Comprehension	B C Learn about Words	D E F Focus on Skills
		1 2 3 4 5	1 2 3 4 5 6 7 8 9 10	1 2 3 4 5 6 7 8 9 10 11 12 13 14 15
		1 2 3 4 5	1 2 3 4 5 6 7 8 9 10	1 2 3 4 5 6 7 8 9 10 11 12 13 14 15
		1 2 3 4 5	1 2 3 4 5 6 7 8 9 10	1 2 3 4 5 6 7 8 9 10 11 12 13 14 15
		1 2 3 4 5	1 2 3 4 5 6 7 8 9 10	1 2 3 4 5 6 7 8 9 10 11 12 13 14 15
		1 2 3 4 5	1 2 3 4 5 6 7 8 9 10	1 2 3 4 5 6 7 8 9 10 11 12 13 14 15
		1 2 3 4 5	1 2 3 4 5 6 7 8 9 10	1 2 3 4 5 6 7 8 9 10 11 12 13 14 15
		1 2 3 4 5	1 2 3 4 5 6 7 8 9 10	1 2 3 4 5 6 7 8 9 10 11 12 13 14 15
		1 2 3 4 5	1 2 3 4 5 6 7 8 9 10	1 2 3 4 5 6 7 8 9 10 11 12 13 14 15
		1 2 3 4 5	1 2 3 4 5 6 7 8 9 10	1 2 3 4 5 6 7 8 9 10 11 12 13 14 15
		1 2 3 4 5	1 2 3 4 5 6 7 8 9 10	1 2 3 4 5 6 7 8 9 10 11 12 13 14 15
		1 2 3 4 5	1 2 3 4 5 6 7 8 9 10	1 2 3 4 5 6 7 8 9 10 11 12 13 14 15
		1 2 3 4 5	1 2 3 4 5 6 7 8 9 10	1 2 3 4 5 6 7 8 9 10 11 12 13 14 15

Answer Keys

Starter 1—Orange
Build Comprehension

A 1. a
2. b
3. a
4. a
5. b

Learn about Words

B 1. mad
2. had
3. glad

C 4. had
5. glad
6. mad

Focus on Skills

D 1. Yes
2. No
3. Yes
4. Yes

Starter 2—Orange
Build Comprehension

A 1. b
2. a
3. b
4. b
5. a

Learn about Words

B 1. name
2. came
3. same

C 4. came
5. name
6. same

Focus on Skills

D 1. started
2. dropped
3. larger
4. pond

Starter 3—Gold
Build Comprehension

A 1. b
2. a
3. b
4. a
5. a

Learn about Words

B 1. get
2. yet
3. met
4. let
5. pet

C 6. met
7. pet
8. yet
9. get
10. let

Focus on Skills

D 1. a
2. b
3. b
4. b

Starter 4—Brown
Build Comprehension

A 1. a
2. a
3. b
4. a
5. b

Learn about Words

B 1. can
2. man
3. ran
4. tan
5. plan

C 6. tan
7. plan
8. can
9. ran
10. man

Focus on Skills

D 1. wrong
2. day
3. stop
4. down

Starter 5—Tan
Build Comprehension

A 1. b
2. b
3. a
4. a
5. b

Learn about Words

B 1. stepladder
2. himself
3. babysit
4. bathroom
5. everyone

C 6. Everyone
7. babysit
8. himself
9. bathroom
10. stepladder

Focus on Skills

D 1. b
2. b
3. a
4. a
5. b

Starter 6—Green
Build Comprehension

A 1. a
2. b
3. b
4. b
5. a

Learn about Words

B 1. sledding
2. slope
3. bunch
4. broad
5. zip

C 6. zip
7. broad
8. Sledding
9. bunch
10. slope

Focus on Skills

D 1. e
2. c
3. b
4. a
5. d

E 6. period
7. question
8. period
9. exclamation
10. question